MASTER BROKERS

INTERVIEWS WITH TOP FUTURES BROKERS

by
John Walsh

The individuals interviewed in this book are not employees of the Chicago Mercantile Exchange®
and their statements and opinions are their own and do not necessarily reflect the views or opinions of
the Chicago Mercantile Exchange.

ISBN 0-915513-61-7

DEDICATION

Maureen, Michael, Kathleen, John, John Jr., and Helen,
your belief in me has helped me believe in myself.

TABLE OF CONTENTS

Other Publications by John Walsh

ABOUT THE PUBLISHER

The Center for Futures Education, Inc. has been working with and training futures brokers since 1981. It has developed several home study courses for futures and securities professionals, including Series 3, Series 7, Series 30 and Series 31 training. The Center's Futures Broker Home Study Course is the most widely used Series 3 preparatory home study course in the futures industry. It is used by companies such as Merrill Lynch, Smith Barney, Dean Witter Reynolds, and PaineWebber, to name a few.

The Center is an independent educational services firm, specializing in teaching and publishing material for the futures industry. Workshops and home study courses are available for complete broker training. The Center is a Commodity Futures Trading Commission (CFTC) authorized Ethics Training provider.

The Center is not in competition with brokerage firms, but acts in support capacity for the futures and securities industries by furnishing quality educational materials, classes, and seminars.

You are welcome to call or write for a free catalog.

Center for Futures Education, Inc.
401 Erie Street, P.O. Box 309
Grove City, PA 16127
(412) 458-5860

Introduction

You have in your hands a book which gives you a first-person account of how sixteen top futures brokers built their businesses.

They all have been extremely generous with their time (many interviews lasted more than five hours) their ideas, struggles, and successes. In these pages, they share their stories with you, explaining what they have learned from their experiences, and gently pass on advice and counsel they firmly believe will help you live up to your potential as a futures broker.

How did the author select the brokers for this book? First, the geographical scope was limited to the United States. Next, we surveyed more than thirty futures industry leaders and asked them for their nominations. If the industry leader worked for a firm that employed brokers, we asked which broker or brokers they would want to hire. Note: we did not permit nominees from the industry leader's own firm. Also, self-nominations were not accepted.

After the survey, we screened more than one hundred brokers. To be included, they had to meet certain basic criteria. They had to have:

1. been in the business at least ten years
2. had no compliance problems
3. significant production
4. a willingness and ability to communicate the specifics of how they get and service clients
5. longevity with one or more firms.

Twenty brokers were interviewed. Of these, sixteen are featured here. We are grateful to all who participated, in whatever capacity, and look forward to working with additional outstanding brokers in the future.

This book is the result of the work of many wonderful people. First, we must thank the Chicago Mercantile Exchange, which came up with the idea, funded the research, and courageously left the selection process for the brokers entirely up to the author. At the risk of leaving someone out, some names must be mentioned for their skill and guidance: Susan O'Toole, Bill Kokontis, Lyn Sennholz, and Jack Schwager.

Finally, we are eternally grateful to all the brokers who gave these often lengthy interviews and then reviewed, modified, cut, added, revised, changed, polished, and re-reviewed more than a total of one thousand pages of manuscript.

One closing note: If you have the name of a top broker who you believe has outstanding ideas to share and meets our criteria, you are welcome to send the name and your reasons for choosing him or her to the Center for Futures Education, Inc. Who knows, we may do *Master Brokers II* someday, and perhaps you or your favorite broker will be in it!

John Walsh

Roy E. Abbott

Refco, Inc.
Minneapolis, Minnesota

Roy, what's your background, please?

Born and grew up in Minnesota. Worked on truck farms as a kid. Picked sweet corn, sold it door to door. After finishing at the University of Minnesota, got a job as a cash grain merchandising trainee at Pillsbury—right here in the Minneapolis Grain Exchange Building. That's over thirty years ago! Mostly did corn and soybeans, some oats. After a couple years, decided to become a stock broker, really liked finance in college. Manager of the stock office said, with my background, "shouldn't you look into being a commodity broker here? The two commodity brokers we had have just retired. We're looking for somebody." So that's what I did and I've been a commodity broker ever since. And my office is still here at the Grain Exchange.

How did you build your business?

Well, looking back, I think my business grew in several different ways. First of all, I was successful in trading, and that's the best way to build a business. I was able to make some money for my clients. I got some referral business that way. Being the only commodity broker in the office also helped. Whenever a cold call came in, I got it. As a matter of fact, I'm still doing business with some of those people from when I started here in 1968.

What's the secret to keeping a client that long?

Well, there are a lot of secrets. Obviously, if we don't make money, they don't survive, so you've got to make them money or help them make money. I think it's a combination. It's working together with them, making them money, keeping them out of trouble. *The biggest problem in this business is getting yourself in a position where you lose so much money that you can't come back from it, and you're not interested in trading anymore.* So steer them in the right direction, keep them out of trouble.

Roy, when I first visited here, I was sure you'd have a private office. Instead, you're sitting right in the middle of all your brokers, right with your troops. Why?

I like to be out with the troops, as you call them. I get a better feel of what's going on, I can hear the orders going in, I know what's going on all the time. I think I have a better feel as a manager for catching problems before they turn into problems, before they turn into big problems. I think the brokers respect me for that. They can come up and ask me a question any time they want to. I'm right here, I'm part of the office really. I set the example. I'm in here at five-thirty, I'm the first one in, and often the last one out, but not always. So I try to set the example.

What is the nature of your book?

I'd say it has changed over time. My book used to be ninety-nine percent speculative. Primarily because of the competitive nature of the business as far as commissions these days, I've gone more to commercial business. Big spec can get the same rate as commercial, but you're running a bigger risk because they can be more of a problem. So if I've got a big spec that will do business for twenty-five dollars and I've got a big commercial that will do business for twenty-five dollars, who am I better off doing business with? Obviously, the commercials. So I've pursued the commercial business more over the last few years and just laid off the spec business. I still have a fairly strong spec business, but I'm pretty much fifty-fifty now, spec versus commercial.

How did you develop your commercial business?

Well, basically you develop the business the same way, regardless of the nature of the accounts. It's through contacts, seminars, cold calls. Most of my business comes through referrals.

Anything else you'd like to add about the nature of your business or book?

I've learned a lot from my customers, and I think that would be one point I'd make to anybody who's coming in to get started. A lot of times your customers, especially when you're just getting started, are going to know a lot more about the market than you do unless you're prospecting greenhorns. Your best prospect is someone who has reason to be in the market either from a speculative or hedging point of view, so they're going to know something about the business. They've been around, they're successful business people more than likely, probably been trading before. They've got knowledge, so I always ask questions of my customers. *"What can you tell me? I want to learn from you.* I don't know anything about. . . How much nitrogen do you have to put in it per acre? How many bushels per acre do you get?"

How would a rookie have a prayer of getting that kind of business?

The key to talking to people like that is you've got to be willing to ask questions. You get the prospect to talk to you, you ask him questions. You don't have to be expert to do business with somebody. *All you have to be able to do is convince him the firm you work for can provide him with the service he needs, the research he needs, and you can help him with those things.* You can't be so aloof that you're the know-it-all. You've got to be able to relate to these people, so you get them talking, you ask them questions.

What kinds of questions do you ask to get your prospects to open up to you?

Well, first of all, you've got to ask them who they are. "What kind of business do you do? Are you a farmer? How many acres do you have? What do you grow? Are you into livestock? Have you ever used the market? Do you hedge, do you speculate? What kind of success have you had?" Just get them going. Farmers love to talk. Once you get them going, it's easy to keep going.

Is this on the phone or in person?

Either way.

What about those not in an ag community?

Well, it's no different. Instead of asking them what they grow, ask them what business they are in. "Tell me something about yourself. Are you interested in taking risks? Do you invest in the stock market? Would you like to look at something that's a little riskier but has a higher reward if you're right?" Common sense, really. Just find out something about that person. They'll tell you what you need to know. It's called qualifying. You qualify the customer or the potential customer. If the guy says "Well, I'm not interested in any risk," you've got the wrong prospect. You go on to the next one because it's a risky deal. You've got to have someone who wants to take a risk over and above the ordinary risk of whatever else they're doing. So it's no different getting them to talk about themselves, it's just asking different kinds of questions.

Did you take sales training or read books on selling?

I didn't do anything other than a couple of these one- or two-day sales training deals, but I didn't spend a lot of time on it. I would certainly recommend to anyone who's coming into this business to spend some time getting sales training. There are plenty of courses around.

What advice do you have for brokers about prospecting?

Well, I think you have to have a plan, and you have to decide whom you're going to prospect. You have to have an idea of what kind of customer you're looking for. In my mind, the customer tends to match the broker. In other words, I like to trade soybeans, I like to trade grains and livestock, so I'm looking for someone with interests in those areas. Then you have to decide how you're going to prospect. You can start with cold calling, which is the worst, time-consuming way to prospect there is, or you can decide to do what I think is the best, put on seminars. I used to do that all the time. I'd get somebody in the local community whom I had some kind of rapport with, either a customer or a friend, something like that. I'd say to them, "Do you have some people out there we can get together with some evening to talk about commodities? I'll come on out and bring some slides and some information and we can have a little get-together." I've spoken in front of two or three people to as many as several hundred. The word gets out you are willing to do these things, and all of a sudden they're calling you. "We're having a marketing meeting. We've got a bunch of farmers who want to talk about the market, can you come out?" "Well, sure I can." So that's the best way to prospect. Then you've got them eyeball-to-eyeball, you can shake their hands, get to know them.

How would people in a non-ag area do this, say in Pittsburgh?

Run an ad in the local paper that you're going to have a meeting at the Holiday Inn and you're going to talk about—you pick your subject—bonds, precious metals, interest rates, whatever. "I'm going to have an expert from my firm come in and talk about it." Advertise in the paper, advertise on the radio. Get a mailing list of people who you think might be good prospects and mail it out. Say, "Would you like to come? If so, return the post card." Then follow up with a call. *Always follow up with a call.* If you make a mass mailing, make sure you call the people a couple of days after you mail it out for that personal touch: "Did you get my letter? Would you be interested in coming?" Most guys will throw it in the basket, but if you call them and it's right there in their hands, "Oh, I might be interested in it." I don't care if it's out in Olivia, Minnesota or Pittsburgh, Pennsylvania. Same kind of deal.

What makes for a good seminar?

Well, the person that's putting it on, obviously. You have to know what you're talking about. You have to pick a subject you feel comfortable talking about; you have to be well-prepared. You have to be able to get up in front of a bunch of people and make a presentation and come off looking good, feeling comfortable about it. The only way to do that is to know your subject. Be able to answer questions afterwards. If you need expert help, have it there. Almost every firm has a research department, and if you call them up to help you with a seminar, most of them will. Then, at least to get started, you watch how they do the seminar, then adapt it to yourself, pick up the style. For example, our research director has been doing seminars for us for twelve years. You watch him do a seminar, and if you can't go out and duplicate that and have a successful seminar, you didn't pay attention. That's the way it goes.

Again, some sales training will fit in nicely with that. At the university, I didn't like English, so I took a class called Communications which got me through the English requirement. It required me to speak in front of groups, which I thought was very good training for me. I didn't know at the time that it would come in handy. Any opportunity you've got to get up and speak in front of people is going to help you. Toastmasters, anything. Get yourself exposed, get out there. When I worked at Piper, they had a radio program, and every time they had a gap when they couldn't find a stockbroker to call, they'd call Roy Abbott. It was always four in the afternoon; they wanted me to be on at seven-thirty in the morning. I always said yes, never turned them down. "Anytime you want me, call me." I'd pick the subject, or let them if they'd insist. It'd be my deal. "This is what I think, this is how I view the market." Never referred to other experts, always to myself. "These are my ideas." It may sound arrogant, but it's not. *You have to come off sounding knowledgeable, but you'd better be because people can tell if you're faking it.*

How did you get knowledgeable and how do you stay knowledgeable?

Well, luckily, I got knowledgeable about grains through my training at Pillsbury. From there I had to train myself in the other things that we traded. It's just a matter of self-education, reading mostly. You find source materials and you read them. Commodity research yearbooks. They always have three or four good articles about different areas of our business. You read everything you can get your hands on, *The Wall Street Journal*, magazines, trade journals, obviously things that affect the currencies and the financials. You're going to get that stuff out of reading *Barron's*, *The Economist*, the *New York Times*, and on and on. We get the Knight Ridder news service in here and there's just constant information regarding things in the business. I read everything that comes across it.

We survey people who've been prospected by brokers but who haven't opened, and we ask them why. One big reason: the broker wasn't knowledgeable. Any comments?

Probably laziness is the biggest weakness. They're not willing to put the time in to acquire the knowledge to come across as knowledgeable.

What are some other ways to prospect, besides seminars?

Well, we talked about cold calling, which I would put at the bottom of the list. Referrals. Between seminars and referrals I'd take referrals any day. Seminars would be number two.

So do you still prospect?

You bet. I'll send research to this guy for a week. I'll call him up and say, "I've been sending you research for a week. Have you been getting it? What do you think of it?" "It's good research!" I know he's going to say it's good research because I know it's good research. Then I'm going to say, "Well, what's your calendar look like? When can I come out and see you?" I'm sure he'll say, "Why not?" I've told him I've been in the business for thirty years, "I do business with big farmers like you, you're the kind of client I want to do business with," so I'll get my butt out there and talk to him.

When you have a prospect you think should be opening, do you ask for the order? How do you "get the check"?

Well, it's a progressive deal and each prospect is different. I think it's kind of like the market, you just have to have a feel for when it's right. When is it right to say, "I'm going to send the papers out, I want to open the account"? From my experience, you lead them in. You tell them, "The next time I've got a real good idea, I'm going to let you know." And when you have a good idea, he's either sent the papers in or he's sitting on them. If he hasn't sent them in, you hit him with the idea, then hopefully it turns out. Then you call back and say, "I've got another good idea. Did you send in those papers?" That's a speculative customer. Now a commercial customer, those guys are tougher to open. It's harder to push the hot button with those guys. They've got people they've been doing business with for a long time, and you've got to work them and work them and work them. You've got to keep on prospecting them. You've got to get them to like you. That takes time. So you just keep working them until you ask them, "Can we open an account, can we do some business?" You've got to be up front and ask them for it. *You don't get business unless you ask for it.* You don't open an account unless you ask for it.

Roy, on the spec side, if you say you have a good idea and it turns out not to be a good idea, then what?

Call them up and say, "The good idea I had was no good, I'm out of it. Changed my mind, took my loss." The quicker the better. They'll respect that because you've told them ahead of time that you're not going to be right all the time. You can't be right all the time in this business, impossible. So if we get into a position that's wrong, we're going to get out of it. So you pre-sell them.

How about servicing an account?

I think every account needs a different level of service and you've got to figure out what that level of service is and provide it. Some people like to be called a lot. Other people don't want to be called a lot, so you've got to know your customer, know what they need, know what they demand, and provide it. It's as simple as that.

How do you find out what they want?

Ask them. They'll let you know. You've got to ask them, "How much service do you want?" I guess that wouldn't be the way I'd phrase it. I'd say, "How often do you want me to call you? What kind of information are you looking for? What kind of information do you want? Do you want a call every half hour? Do you want a call when I see something happening that's important? Give me an idea where you're coming from." A lot of times in this business you get called by a customer as many times as you're calling them. Especially in this day and age, if you have a serious client, they've got their own equipment, eighty percent of them. Didn't used to be that way. Now, something starts to happen, the lights light up, you haven't got time to grab all the calls. They're all on the phone. It's a lot different.

How about honesty?

My philosophy has always been that you've got to be one hundred percent honest in this business. You can't cut corners, period. I don't believe in it, I don't allow it. If I catch a broker lying, I'll fire him. I just don't believe in it. I mean if you make an error for a customer, you eat it immediately. You take your errors. One hundred percent honesty, no corners cut, period.

Can you give some examples of honesty or gray areas?

I would say in the area of prospecting, it's telling a client something, making him believe you know something that you don't, or that you are more knowledgeable than you are. That's plain B.S. My approach to that has always been, "If I don't know, I'm going to tell you, and then I'm going to tell you I'll find out. What you want to know that I don't know, I'll find out and get back to you." I don't B.S. prospects because most of them know right away when they're being B.S.ed, and if they're dumb enough to be B.S.ed, you probably don't want them for customers anyway. Let's be honest about it. Why be anything but honest? It just doesn't make sense. If you B.S. somebody one day, you have to B.S. him the next day. Pretty soon you're caught up in this trap and it's just not worth it.

What about goals?

Well, I think goal-setting is an ongoing process. I think it's almost impossible to set the goal that you may ultimately reach the first time you set goals. So, you sit down, you set realistic goals for yourself, knowing what you know about yourself and what you're getting into at that point in time, and then you make adjustments as you go along.

How about listening?

I think if you're going to be a good salesman, you've got to be a good listener. *It all comes down to this: you can't open an account unless you're willing to listen to the prospect, to find out what his needs are so you can determine if he's a good prospect.* If he is, you have to tell him how you and your company can meet and fill his needs, so you've got to be a really good listener.

How do you become a good listener?

First of all, you have to decide that other people have knowledge and are worth listening to. Some brokers have the attitude that they know everything so they don't have to listen. I never thought I was that smart. I think you've got to be humble enough to listen to people, to what they say, to learn from them. It's another one of those personality traits. You can't be so pompous and so in love with yourself that you can't listen to other people *and hear what they're saying.* You can learn an awful lot from people just by listening. Let them talk. Don't overpower them with your own blabber. I hear that so many times: the broker just won't let the customer talk. *Shut up! Let the customer do the talking.* Ask questions, listen. There's always something you can learn. *The more insecure the broker, the less he listens, the more he talks. He has to prove how smart he is because he really, down deep, doesn't feel too smart.*

How about work habits? What are the work habits of the successful brokers you've seen?

I can only speak from my own point of view. I get in early because if you want to stay informed in this business, you have to be here early. There's so much information that comes out overnight. It takes me a good hour-and-a-half of reading in the morning to get through the stuff that happened overnight. You've got to spend a lot of time keeping yourself informed. It's not an eight-to-three or -four job. It's a lot longer than that if you want to be successful.

Any other work habits?

You have to have an organized prospecting effort. I think that's very important. You've got to be a good phone person. You've got to stay on the phone. This is a phone business. You've got to be on it all the time. You've got to like to talk to people. You've got to be a salesman, a trader, a money manager.

How about older, more experienced, once-successful brokers who are now floundering?

I'd tell them to look at what they were doing when they were successful and try to repeat it, try to do those things. Now maybe they've lost the ability to do that. Everybody grows old and we lose our ability to do things at peak performance. It happens to everybody. So, I guess they've got to say to themselves, "Have I lost my ability to do what I did when I was successful?" If they have lost that ability, then maybe they need to decide to do something else, but first they go back and examine what they did when they were successful. What were they doing? Try to do it again. It's easy to get into bad habits, and they've got to keep going back and talking to themselves, "Hey, I'm making mistakes, I'm doing something wrong here." I bowl every week, and I see people who bowl a five hundred series and the next week it's three hundred. It's because they're not being consistent and they're not doing the same thing over and over again. Brokers who were once successful and now aren't are not doing what they were doing when they were successful. They have to get back there and do it right. It's just that simple. Deep down, they know how; they've done it before. They can do it again if they're willing to pay the price.

Just a couple more questions. If you had three pieces of advice to give to new brokers, what would you give?

Work hard. Be honest. Try to learn the rules of the business.

Anything we didn't cover you'd like to add?

Find somebody who can help you when you've got a problem. Don't try to be macho and go it alone. If you've only been around two or three years, you don't know all the ins and outs of the business. Find somebody you can go to. Get some help, get some advice. Say, "Here's the deal, what do I do?" Don't be afraid to ask for it!

Anything else?

Your biggest enemy is yourself in this business. Human nature is such that nobody likes to admit they're wrong, and in this business, you have to be willing to admit you're wrong. That's why I say your biggest enemy is yourself. It's human nature not to be willing to admit when you're wrong. Take your lumps. Take your medicine. *The first loss is always the smallest.* So you're always really fighting human nature, fighting yourself.

Your son, Mike, works for you as a broker. What would you like him to know about the business when you're not around?

Mike, don't lose sight of the things I've said here. If you remember the things that make you successful and keep doing them, you'll be all right. It's when you forget the things that make you successful that everything can go to hell. In our business, you can't go out and practice, like football, so you always keep the rules in mind, go over them, do whatever you need to do to keep yourself on the right track. Mike, you've got to have inner strength. It's got to come from someplace inside. A person either has that kind of strength to draw on or they don't. You have it. At times, you'll have to give yourself that little speech I give myself, "I've done it before, I can do it again. Let's get to work, let's do it!" The opportunities are always there. You just have to be smart enough, good enough, and work hard enough to take advantage of them. And, oh yes, one last thing, Mike. *Don't let mistakes get you down. They're part of our business. They're part of any business. Yesterday is gone. We trade futures here!*

Kim Barley

Orlando, Florida

Kim, tell us a little about your background, please.

I was born in Jacksonville, Florida and grew up in Orlando. I earned a degree in agriculture from the University of Florida, got out of the army in 1953, and sold fertilizer for my father, plants and flowers with my father-in-law. I got into the securities business in 1961 to get an overview of the possible industries in which to build a career. I found out I liked the futures industry, and I'm still in it today. I was fortunate to find something that was right for me early in my career.

How can brokers who may be struggling tell if a career in futures is for them?

Well, as you know, there's a pretty high mortality rate among futures brokers. So first of all, they have to really like the business. If they've been in the business for a year or two and are still struggling, they should re-examine whether they should be in the business. I would seek out a successful broker and see if he or she would be my mentor. I'd examine the work habits and the prospecting methods of successful brokers. I'd find out how they service their clients. Then I'd put in at least as much effort as these brokers did when they were building their business—not only then, but as much work as they continue to put in. Then I'd give myself another chance. If I weren't successful then, I'd look for something different to do. Too many brokers blame their lack of success on the markets. They have to ask themselves, "Why is it that the successful brokers in our business do well no matter what the markets are doing?"

How did you start your commodity business?

Well, this is Orange Country, and I was one of the few guys who started doing orange juice from the beginning. It's probably like any new contract of today. We had to learn the orange juice business from the growers and processors. We didn't understand hedging, so we had to learn it first and then teach the trade. We found out early what we discovered time and again—the traders didn't want to hedge: they wanted to speculate. So we spent literally thousands of hours educating the traders over the years, teaching them all about hedging, what basis is, how the market functions— all the stuff any good broker would do when trying to break into a market.

We wrote dozens of papers, spoke at seminars, meetings, conventions, even helped put together a booklet about hedging orange juice. Sandra Kaul actually wrote it—we provided the information. We've given it away by the hundreds. It's helped establish us as experts in the orange juice business, but none of it happened overnight. It was tough getting started.

After we got the O.J. business up and running, we hired a couple of good brokers from up north to come down and take it over because the firm wanted me to be a full-time manager. After several years, I decided I didn't want to be the branch manager anymore—maybe the decision was mutual—and I decided to go back into production again.

How did you get started the second time?

Well, I don't think it was any easier than the first time, but nothing's really easy in this business. Other people in the office were already doing the orange juice business, so I had to go after something else. At that time, the cattle business in Florida was being overlooked from a hedging perspective. The guys down here knew how to grow animals, but they didn't know how to sell them or protect themselves from supply and demand and, most of all, prices.

Now, here's the difference, I believe, between myself and a lot of other brokers who simply would not want to do the work and spend the time. First, people weren't hedging cattle, and many brokers would say, "It's too tough to change these ranchers because they don't hedge. Their fathers and their grandfathers didn't hedge, and you're not going to change the minds of these people because they're too tough, too stubborn, and too set in their ways." You see, most brokers won't even consider the fact that maybe they themselves weren't smart enough or persistent enough or good enough salesmen. *It's always easier to blame the prospect when you don't make the sale.*

We also had another barrier to overcome before we could get these people to hedge their cattle. We had an uphill battle because they didn't raise heavy feeders here. They raised light feeders which they then shipped out west in the winter to fatten up and finish out there. That was another negative about getting into this business, but we didn't let that stop us.

I studied all the historical and statistical data available. When all that work was done, I started traveling the state just trying to get people to listen. I knocked on a lot of cowboys' back doors.

How did you survive while you were doing all this "missionary" work? Weren't you tempted to get these cowboys to speculate a little, just so you could make a few commission dollars?

The firm agreed to pay me a salary for a year. Even after that year, I've never looked at this as a "who do I need to call to get an order to make a commission?" business. I have my own philosophy about this business.

What is your philosophy about this business?

I think that I'm a partner with whomever I'm doing business, or I try to be. That can be a hindrance because some people just want me to take orders and execute and be done with it, but I really like the involvement of being on their board, on their trading committee. I've always felt if you provide people with good information, good timing, and back away from the selling aspect of it, the business will come. The business comes when people know you are doing for them what you think is right—though that doesn't necessarily make you right. The market makes you right or wrong, but if the decision is made correctly from a hedging perspective, that's good.

I don't actively seek speculation business. That's a tough, tough business. Realistically, the only way to do spec business is to manage it yourself, and that takes on a whole new dimension. We have people in the firm who do that and make a lot of money, but I talked with those guys, and they have the same perspective: if you're a spec trader, always look to the long-term trade, always look for the position trade, always use money management, and stay away from trying to short-term day trade because it's a killer.

The speculators I do have are basically those guys who are looking for long-term position trades.

You mentioned that you knocked on a lot of doors, went to see a lot of people. What was that like?

The first thing I realized is that really good accounts take a long time to get. I used to think that the more times I'd get thrown out of an office, the better it was because it gave me the initiative to go knock on the door again. It took me literally years to get accounts. These were substantial accounts, but it took me years. I took the attitude that the only way to really develop good business was to first do the work to really understand their business. *Then it was critical to go call on them in person, not on the phone.* I only used the phone to get an appointment. Never to try to get a trade.

I made myself a flip-chart presentation. It was an easy way for me to give a presentation because the prospect had to go through all the flips. This kind of legwork leads to good things. You get good exposure, but you must make a good presentation, and to do so you have to do your homework. You really have to understand what you're doing or they'll see through it in a minute and won't touch you. I felt from the early days that I had to be prepared, I had to have a business plan, I had to have a plan about whom I wanted to see. I went to all the cattle conventions, all the hog-producers' conventions, just for exposure, so that when I phoned for an appointment, I could say, "Oh, I met you at the convention, may I come see you?"

You mentioned conventions. How much time, effort, and money do you think a broker should spend on this kind of education?

I think commercial brokers should go to their relevant conventions. My bills—entertainment, education, computer hardware and software, conventions, books, tapes, and subscriptions—run in the vicinity of twenty thousand a year. I pay it all out of my own pocket, and I don't object to paying. I'm in a very specialized business—no one can just walk in and do this business. Commercial futures is a highly specialized business. I call that a franchise, and I'm going to protect that franchise.

Any other advice to brokers about how to build their business?

Early on, when I was selling plants and things, I realized I didn't know how to sell, so I took every course I could. I can remember hiring a professor at the university to come down and teach my staff when I became a sales manager for my father-in-law's nursery. I brought him in to teach my guys and then I learned myself. *I learned to listen, not to what people are saying to me, but what they're telling me.* There's a very big difference in that.

I'm trying to teach this to the young man who works with me now. I always listen to what they're telling me, not to what they're saying. I think that aspect of trying to discern what customers needs are, what they really want you to do, is how you make the beginning of the relationship work, and how you become a partner with them in what they're doing.

How do you read people?

I've had some training, but I've learned to watch how people react to what I say. If they move their eyes away, they're not hearing me. So eye-contact, mannerisms, how they look, if they look guarded—all these are important to notice. Also, when he's on this side of the desk and I'm on that side of the desk, he's in control. So I have to try to get it to where, when we are together, he doesn't sit behind the desk.

Where did you learn that kind of stuff?

Time, you know, and like I said, I've read a lot of books on sales-manship, a lot of books on psychology in selling and that type of thing. Some of it you just learn if you're observant and you watch. I always self-critique every sales call: "What'd I do right? What'd I do wrong?"

Even as long as you've been in this business, you still evaluate a sales call?

Always. There's a lot of negative selling in business today. People bad-mouthing one firm and another. It's very unprofessional. You only tear yourself down when you're tearing someone else down. As competitive as I am with other orange juice brokers in our industry—we'll kill each other trying—we respect each other. I never feel too badly if I lose a customer to one of my competitors. It just means he did a better job than I did and I have to work that much harder to get that customer back.

And do you get them back?

You bet. Well, as many as I can.

How do you prospect? Any advice?

A broker is continually prospecting, whether he knows it or not. If he's not doing a very good job servicing his accounts, word gets around, particularly in commercial business, but in spec, too. That's negative prospecting. People like to talk. If you're on the golf course too much, or don't return calls in a timely manner, or party too hard at trade shows, or behave in a boorish manner, or dozens of other behaviors, you're doing negative prospecting.

I'm always prospecting, but I don't bombard people with phone calls. *I've prospected some people for as long as five years.* One way I maintain 'value-added' contact with prospects is to fax them our reactions and ideas every morning or whenever I need to. *Just like in trading, you must be patient in prospecting.* In the meantime, I have to service the account, not with trades, but with information, advice, charts if they want them, feedback, market data, industry news. I'm always trying to meet their needs. Find a need and fill it better than your competition. If I can't bring something to the party, I don't deserve to be at the party.

Kim, any other advice about prospecting?

New or experienced brokers can increase their chances of success if they focus, if they specialize. The more you specialize, the better job you can do for your customers. I think a broker has to decide if he is going to concentrate primarily on the hedging business or on the speculative business. Also, what you need to do in this business, hedge or spec, is not to worry about the commissions. The commissions will follow the success.

Kim, when we survey clients and prospects, many of them complain that the broker doesn't listen. Any comments?

You know, that's a tough one because the broker thinks he's supposed to give the customer an edge, supposed to tell them something. I've found that in my younger days I was more aggressive. *I told them what I thought and if they didn't think the way I did, of course, they were wrong!*

I had to change my attitude because, as I mentioned earlier, I wanted my relationships with my clients to be partnerships; therefore, what we're really after is a consensus about what we're doing. To solve my "ego problem" and to help create consensus,

I came up with this phrase which I still use constantly when talking with my clients: *"Let's share what we think about things today."* If they want to go first I always let them, and if you listen, really listen, the other guy will eventually give you a chance. Just don't be too anxious to make your point.

Any other advice for young brokers?

It's a lot easier to keep an account than to get a new one. We all may have a few customers who aren't that happy with us, and we usually know who they are. It's a good idea to ask your customers once in a while how you're doing. Ask them if there is anything you can do to serve them better.

A couple weeks ago, I had this feeling that a certain customer felt maybe we weren't partnering with him as well as we could be. My "daytime wife"—my trading assistant Sandy—who is very sensitive, very aware, sensed this, too. She felt something wasn't just right and said, "You know, Kim, you had better go see him." So I took a Friday afternoon and went to his place and sat down with him. Rocked on the porch with him, if you will. I told him about my feelings, my concerns, then gave him a chance to get a few things off his chest and tell me the problems he was having with us. *He felt we weren't really listening to him and we were miscommunicating. This can easily happen if a broker is pushing his agenda at the expense of a customer's needs or wants, or if his agenda is at cross purposes with the customer's agenda.* In time you'll get your chance to speak, but maybe not that day. You have to be patient. Anyway, I said, "Let's get things straight, let's clear the air because I don't want anything to interfere with our doing business together." After he told me his concerns I said, "We'll get right to it and see if we can't improve." He liked that.

Kim, you may not want me to bring this up, but what about your commissions?

John, I believe I'm the highest-priced commissioned broker in orange juice there is. Sometimes I get concerned about it, so I ask my customers and they say they aren't concerned. I mentioned earlier about bringing something to the party—"value-added," if you will. If you bring something to the party, you'll be paid accordingly. If you don't bring something to the party, you'll be paid accordingly.

How do you handle the stress in this business?

I used to find it stressful because I allowed customers in the early days to have huge positions in adverse times. I have since learned that managing the money is the most important thing, and if you manage the money, you obviously don't carry huge positions without adequate resources. I'm trying to hedge products. So I always have to look at the short side of the market; therefore, I always have to be kind of bearish. Now what are we trying to do in agriculture to be more profitable? Before we hedge we have to know what kind of market we're in: if we're in a bull market we never hedge; if we're in a bear market we need to double up. Now, you can't realistically do that, but what you can do is buy insurance to protect yourself on the down side. The biggest mistake people make in this business is not understanding basis. I've also seen people try to buy the price instead of the basis. That's common across all industries, not just O.J. Those who wait for the price will lose the basis, profit, and the price.

What have you learned from your failures?

Lots of things, really. *I learned about being a loud mouth.* I learned that when you were "always right," those situations became failures because you're not always right. I have had to retrain myself to learn that I can't be everything to everybody. Whether the customer thought he was right or wrong about what happened is not important. You see, we're back to something I've tried to stress all the way through, and that is, you try to build relationships with customers, then you build communications, then you build service—and that's the important ingredient. In order for your business to have any depth, any staying power, the relationship must come first—which means the customer comes first!

Thanks for your help, Kim. Is there anything else you'd like to add?

Let's be very basic. When God created man, he created him for relationships and fellowship, and I think if you have that in your business, then you have everything.

Douglas E. Carper

J.C. Bradford & Co.
Lincoln, Nebraska

Could you please tell us a little about yourself, Doug?

I grew up in northeast Nebraska on a small farm which is still a family farm (a regular grain and livestock farming operation), the oldest of five children, majored in ag economics at the University of Nebraska. I had to work my way through school and found myself engaged to be married. I didn't do well enough at school to consider going on to graduate school, but I'd had some success in part-time sales jobs and that gave me a little confidence about trying this business. It seemed natural for me to get into the commodities business.

How did you know about commodities?

Well, I had taken a class at the university in agricultural marketing, and we had a professor who is well-known in this area for teaching the basics of hedging. We actually even had a make-believe trading class where we were allocated a certain amount of paper money for trading and so forth. I didn't necessarily do well in that, but it piqued my interest.

How did you grow your business?

I wrote down the name of every person or large producer I would have reason to call, and I called them. I had to be pretty creative. Also, to be taken seriously at twenty-three was a challenge.

So what did you do when you started?

You just start. You begin to look for people to do business with. Number one, they've got to hear from you. They're not going to take you very seriously because you don't have the wisdom or the experience, but you've got to somehow convey to them your seriousness. I made the commitment, of course we had fewer markets at that time, to really become immersed in understanding their basic businesses, whether it was cattle feeder, grain farmer, corn farmer, or whatever. You need to be around your prospects. So I made a commitment to start going to trade association conventions and seminars, and tried to rub shoulders with these people as a contemporary, rather than as a salesman. The first thing I had to do was build some credibility for myself in the markets I was breaking into. I had to learn the jargon and the industry. You can try to talk about the markets, but if you can't relate it to a prospective client, you aren't going to be taken seriously. You have to somehow gain your prospects' confidence that you understand their unique needs or interests.

How did you gain prospects' confidence?

Well, I had a farm background, so that was a great start, and I was sitting here in the middle of the western part of the corn belt, and we have large-scale operations in Nebraska.

Did you just go knock on doors?

That's when cold calling really did work. So I would work, in the early years, more often than not four nights a week, and I was at the office until late at night making cold calls.

Cold calls to get them to open an account or what?

Basically to introduce myself, to talk to people about the markets, and to say, "Yes, absolutely I'm interested in doing business with you. What do you think of the corn market? What do you think of the cattle market?" That was a time when futures were foreign to a lot of producers, and a lot of people were really afraid of them. We had exciting markets then, too; at least people would talk to you. So eventually I had excellent reception from people because, even though I was twenty-three years old, I was able to get on the phone and talk intelligently about their businesses. I knew what it was like to live on a farm, I knew the kinds of things that were going through their minds, and I enjoyed the process of developing a network with people. The truth of the matter is, I was able to be in the loop with people in businesses right away. I was talking about the markets, I was learning on the fly. I wasn't necessarily qualified at the time, but neither were they. People were generally receptive and I made a lot of phone calls. I knew, growing up on the farm, that trying to call somebody in the middle of the day was a lost cause because they were outside doing work. Occasionally, you'd catch them at the noon hour, or maybe very early in the morning. That's one alternative. Since I couldn't work all the time, I generally opted to make phone calls from around seven to nine in the evening. When it got to be nine o'clock central time I knew that I could call the western time zone and talk for an hour more out there. In western Nebraska, they were an hour behind us. It was great to be able to develop a network of contacts. Then I'd send them some materials or copies of charts.

Can a young person do that today?

Not as easily. Rather than a shotgun approach where you can scatter and see what sticks, today's marketing has to be a little more sophisticated because the audience is more sophisticated. You're not able to get in to talk to people like you could in the past because, after all, there are so many other marketers out there vying for their attention. So what it amounts to today is that young people can do it, but they have to work on the relationship more than I had to.

How can young brokers develop relationships?

They still can join the trade associations. They can still spend time out of the office, as opposed to spending more time in the office. They need to spend more time face-to-face with individuals, gaining some trust in the relationship.

How can they get those appointments?

Very few appointments can be made with a cold call unless there's some natural sphere of influence, so they're going to have to go out and network with individuals in a particular area of our business, and then use that as an avenue of credibility. You have to be a lot more polished, and not necessarily clever, but you're going to have to be more knowledgeable these days for a face-to-face meeting, and I think that's probably a blessing in disguise.

How so?

Well, if I had a fault, it was that I had reasonable success early on, and I found it was easy for me to do business by phone. I could talk on the telephone, I wasn't afraid of it, and it was easy for me to use. So I didn't go out to see many people in person; however, I always dealt with a lot of trade associations and saw a lot of people that way, and then I'd call them on the phone. At least I met them once, briefly usually. To develop a closer relationship, you'll have a better chance if you can meet people face-to-face.

Okay, again, how can a young broker get enough people to see him face-to-face?

The way I look at it is, if life insurance agents—the oldest game in the town—can continue to get in to see people and the best thing they're doing is selling them a benefit that only helps them when they die, it seems to me a futures broker can get in if he tries and if he calls enough people; but if he doesn't believe in his product, he's going to have a hard time. If he honestly gets excited about these markets, it translates into enthusiasm, and people will see it.

How do brokers find a product that they can get enthusiastic about if their experience has been that they've lost five thousand dollars for each of their first several accounts?

I think they just have to realize the possibilities, and not be so hard on themselves. If somebody comes in and puts down five thousand dollars to trade commodities and the first thing he does is want to trade every single day or over-trade, it's not the market's fault he loses money. It's because of the inevitable, over-leveraged, too-frequent trading. Too many people are impatient and not very practical about it. So what these brokers have to do is understand it's not their fault necessarily if a customer loses money, even if they made the recommendation. There's another train that runs by every ten minutes. They need to keep coming back with more ideas. That's what the business is. The profits will take care of themselves.

The losses are what you have to manage, and I think that a lot of people, including myself, invest a lot of time and energy in getting too committed to a particular idea. The idea may be great, but it may not take place tomorrow or the next day or the next month. So I think the key thing for young brokers today is, if they're going to deal with retail investors, they must have a well-defined, businesslike approach, including the prospects' needs and objectives along with things like patience and money management. Those are the first things that need to be discussed. I think they've got to sell that story. The reason people get involved in commodities is because they can take a small amount of money and conceivably make a lot of money. That story is powerful enough that they keep coming back to it repeatedly. If a guy puts five thousand dollars up and loses it all on one trade, does that mean commodities trading is bad? No, it means that trade didn't work or he had too many contracts on or whatever. It takes constant self-analysis to realize this. If you want to get beaten up, if you like being whipped, you can constantly be down-in-the-mouth in this business if you want to. You'll figure out, possibly subconsciously, how to make yourself miserable. Historically, if you look at people in the brokerage business, many are negative. They think the customers are dumb and everyone's dumb. This breeds mediocrity and under-performance.

So now a broker is enthusiastic about the markets and his product and he's making the calls and he's going out to see people. When he gets in front of somebody, what should she or he do?

If we're talking about the retail broker, I think the first thing you've got to do is somehow make it clear to the prospect that you're not going to hit and run, that you're here to give him a specific prescription. No guarantees, of course, but you're not going to leave this guy high and dry. The prospect wants to be assured that the firm he's dealing with is solid, that you're solid, not a flake. You develop some kind of relationship on the basis of trust, and you've got some kind of specific action plan. You must assure your prospects you're going to be their eyes and ears and their guide. People will be receptive to commodity trading if you can somehow convince them you're going to be there through thick and thin, and that they can be involved in commodities in a sound businesslike manner—and that you've got a game plan in a specific area. There will be other trades you might approach them about later, but I do think that you have to go to them with a specific idea. If nothing else, it will show them you know something. I find, if you can articulate a well-thought-out concept, a lot of people will open an account.

Doug, you always look like you stepped out the pages of *Gentleman's Quarterly*. Do you have a philosophy about personal appearance?

Well, there are different opinions about that. When you're in Rome, do as the Romans do. I think there's a little bit of that. You have to be careful not to talk down to your prospect. You've got to use some basic sales techniques that make sense. *You have to look like a successful person.* I always attempt to dress reasonably well, have a nice office, look like I'm not frazzled, like I'm in control of my faculties, and like I have a solid, methodical approach to doing business. A lot of people get enthusiastic about the markets, for example, and that's fine, but when they go out to see the prospect, they look like they're on the verge of a nervous breakdown. You can't do that. Most people's investment horizons aren't that way. So you have to give them a calm, comforting feeling, that in this exciting opportunity and in this environment that provides for it, you're a guiding light. You must give the impression you're professional, that you're going to be around for awhile. If you don't value your reputation, your image, no one else will. So you have to look like it. That means going through the motions. If you can't afford it, fine, but at least look neat, well-scrubbed, and relatively successful. *No one wants to do business with somebody who looks as though he's broke.*

Any more advice to brokers about prospecting?

The first place is brokers' natural spheres of influence. They can conduct small seminars. They can go out and invite people. Mailing is, I think, a waste of time. I'm pretty much opposed to it. I think rifle-shot approaches of cold calling still work. I think you have to arrange for lunch, and I think you have to stop by and say, "I want to spend fifteen minutes of your time." You'll be surprised, if you keep hammering away, how you'll make contacts, but you need to promote your business in your everyday life. That's nothing new. What that means is, if you're playing golf or if you're in the community, join Jaycees or Kiwanis. Young people need to be active, need to be around. Maybe they're involved in politics. People who are ideological tend to congregate. If you're an active in politics, you start going to the party functions; before you know it, you're a contemporary with these people. They're likeminded. You become known.

And what would you say to them when you called them up?

It was easy for me to call and say, "I'm with so and so, and the reason I'm calling is that I'm in the grain business. I know that you're a big corn producer and I want to talk to you about the corn market."

Another approach I've used is: "John you probably don't know who I am, but I'm with XYZ Commodities, and I'm in the investment business. I'd like to talk with you about a special situation. You've probably never been involved in it, and if you've ever heard anything about it, it's probably been negative, and for most people that's probably correct; but I'd like to tell you about a situation." A lot of times they won't let you make the appointment, so you've got to tell them right then and there that there's a situation you think makes some sense. "If you have some interest in it, I'd like to get together with you." Or "I'd like to drop something in the mail to you." And if nothing happens from it, fine—and tell him that. Chances are he'll never remember what you mailed him if he ever does business with you, but if it does work, you can call back and say, "Look, I talked to you about six months ago and. . . ." Same story. I think you've got to make it clear to people what the economics are. Make a few salient points. Give them some facts. They'll find them interesting. "I'd like to talk to you about that. It's simply, I think, an investment opportunity for the right kind of businesslike plan." You've got to give them comforting terms like that and a sound, businesslike approach—and "I'm going to show you. . . ." "You may not have any interest whatsoever, but you'll be smarter." Entrepreneurs, that's the way they operate; they like to know what's going on, to be *in the know*.

How do you find entrepreneurs to prospect, to phone for in-person appointments?

You've got to get to know people. *You just can't go to work and go home and shut the door.* You've got to be interested. Also, one of the things I always do is get to know something about somebody first, from an article, for example. This is a trade publication, *Blank Magazine.* On the cover is Joe Doe, Anytown, USA. Now, you've got to have something of an ego to let your mug be on the front page of this magazine, so he's approachable. He may talk to you about the fact he's on the cover, don't you agree?

Absolutely.

So you talk to people and say, "Look, I read this article in *Blank Magazine*." Number one, he knows that you're reading *Blank Magazine*, you know something about his trade, or if it's the trucking business, you say, "Look, I've been involved," say you're doing business in oil and gas, and you say, "Look, I came across something in the *Nebraska Trucker*."

Just the fact you've read the *Nebraska Trucker*.

Yeah, all of a sudden it piques his interest. He doesn't say, "Are you looking for prospects?" He might think that, but instead you say you're calling because you've seen his picture in the magazine, and you go from there. I think what you do with these people is, you find out who they are with, who are other successful people in their company. Then maybe you get the name of the CFO or whoever's in charge of hedging their oil and gas exposure. That's the audience you target, that's who you want to do business with, and at least in my case, *I felt it was just as easy to talk to somebody who was successful as someone who wasn't.* So, I think young people have to be adaptable: as they get more confidence they'll be able to call on people who are owners of businesses; they've got to find the people who have reputations as risk-takers in general. Again, think about the marketing approach. You can wear yourself out if all you do is send mass mailings out of the office. It can fool you, you think you're keeping busy.

I think the problem with mass mailing in general is this revolution in computerized mailing programs and mass marketing. Here's what you're competing against: with desktop publishing, Joe Shmoe can operate out of his garage and look like he's a Fortune 500 company with just a few clicks of the mouse button, so no one believes good-looking stuff anymore. If you have a huge budget and you're supersophisticated, maybe you can make it work, but the failure of mailings is enormous. So I think you try rifle-shot approaches. If you're going to do some mailing, if you're going to send out twenty-five, make absolutely sure that you follow up with a personal call or contact. Maybe even visit them. Knock on the door and say, "Look, I sent you a letter and. . . ."

You mean just show up at their office?

Yes, exactly. Just say, "I dropped you a line here the other day, I don't know if you had a chance to look at it, but here's a copy of it. I happened to be in your building and I wanted to say, 'Hi.' I know you must get tons of mail, you probably threw it away, but while I'm here, if you have ten, fifteen minutes, no more than that. . . ." You need to carefully cultivate your mailing list and work it and work it. When you're mass marketing and you've got five hundred letters you're sending out, there's no way for you to be personal, except by accident. So I think as you become more sophisticated, you need to build on what works in the securities business. Take chapter and verse from them and from the insurance business. It's a relationship business, and we should approach it that way. Now if you want to do it as a mass marketing business, be prepared to do business for nothing. We live in an era of Wal-Marts, KMarts, mass marketing, direct marketing, yet the securities business has done extremely well over the last ten years, mostly because of the markets, but also because they've developed a sophisticated marketing approach for their brokers. Generally speaking, the securities firms have attracted good salespeople, and they've worked on cultivating relationships.

Doug, there's a category of brokers out there called untracked veterans. Some were million-dollar producers in the eighties and they're dying today. What advice do you have for veterans who were big producers but now are starving?

I'm starving, so let's talk about that. [Orders sandwiches.] Number one, they should take some stock in the fact they were successful during the eighties, and they're in a transition period. If they were successful in the eighties, they were doing something good, they brought something to the party—but now that they're struggling, they need to wake up and smell the coffee, and realize that they've got a fundamental choice here. They made a lot of money in the eighties and they can either quit or, if they want to stay in the business, they have to realize that, as always, commodity trading is in a constant state of change. They need to reinvent, reacquaint themselves with the girl they brought to the dance, and stop being intimidated by all of the doom-and-gloomers in our business.

There are a lot of them. An awful lot of them. Many offices I go into, "Oh, it's never been worse. There's no money out there." You mentioned positive attitude. Could you talk about that?

Well, the biggest factor that comes to mind is that a lot of individuals out here today forget why they're in the business. They're waiting for the phone to ring and they're in the Wal-Mart mentality of "The business will come to me." They forget that unless they're doing it like Charles Schwab, the only reason people do business with you is because of *you*, *you're* bringing something to the party—and either it's great service or research ideas or a soothing hand.

They need to tighten up the belt a little bit and begin to do what they've always done in the past, except modify it. Change their approach. They don't necessarily have to be intimidated. I think the time has come when conventional transactional business is going to have some appeal again.

But these guys, I'll say to them, "Do you have a marketing plan?" "No." "Do you ever go out to see anybody?" "No, I don't do that." "Do you have anything written down as to what you're going to do tomorrow or next week or next month?"

That's right. The big disadvantage for the young guy is, he doesn't have any experience. He has a hard time breaking the ice, but if you are in the business with ten or more years experience, that in itself—if you can make that clear to people—they respect that. Just ask yourself how many people you know have been at a job for a long time. So they need to leverage their experience. At forty-four, I want to leverage my experience. So I think that what these individuals have to pursue is a positive, upbeat attitude: "I've been in this business a long time, I know a lot about the markets." Give them some historical perspective. Give them a little wisdom. It's a more sophisticated marketing approach, but it's also élitism—and I think that élitism will sell, too. Very few people have been called by a commodity broker who's been in the business fifteen years.

Very few people are approached professionally. It can be flattering. If a successful individual picks up the phone and says, "Listen, you've probably never had reason to talk to me before. I've never called you, but I know you're a successful person. I've been in the business for fifteen years. I've got a pretty good memory about the financial markets. We've had a very good stock market, and a very good bond market until this past year. You know these things, I don't need to tell you, but there's a situation developing in the grain markets that I think has major significance and I'd like to talk to you about it—take a few minutes of your time, or send you something in the mail." You've got to give them a reason. Now people may say, "I have no interest in this," and you say, "That's fine," but by the fact that you've been around for fifteen years, something significant's in the offing. The way I look at it is, probably in most cases they just need to get off their rear ends.

I'm going to mention some words. The first one is *discipline*. What does the word *discipline* mean to you as far as being successful in our business?

Two things. One, of course, is the discipline of the way you solicit for trades, in that you've got to be objective with the client. You've got to know when to fold a particular trade and go on to the next plan, and you've got to have that discipline to realize that taking care of the losses is first and foremost. The profits will take care of themselves if you keep on the game plan. No great pearls of wisdom there, but it's generally conceded by most that you've got to be disciplined not to have a wreck on your hands. *A lot of people who get burned trading commodities, their biggest single problem is that they've invested too much time and energy into something with no backup plan if it didn't work.* I think what happens is that a lot of people do that. It doesn't work and then they blow their clients out, and they have to start all over again. So *discipline* to me is that you follow the basic rules, that means managing the risk for a client to meet his needs. The other discipline is basic regimen in schedule.

Talk about discipline in a broker's schedule, please.

Everyone has his own general approach, but you need to at least be committed to putting in a full day. That doesn't necessarily mean being chained to your desk, but you've got to make a commitment, if you're a transactional broker especially, to being here during the market hours, or at least in a position where you know what's going on, that you're in the loop. That's what people are paying you for. Go see people after the markets close and on weekends and exchange holidays, if appropriate. You've got to have good work habits. You've got to be willing to put in the time and energy. The harder I work the luckier I get. I think that's the name of the game here. People have to have a discipline of standing up at the plate and continuing to take pitches. Sooner or later you're going to put it over the fence or you're going to put a few singles out in the infield. You can't do that if you're not there to do it, and I think a lot of people in this business lack the tenacity to stay in the trenches. Whether it's servicing their clients or whether it's prospecting doesn't make any difference.

The next word or, rather phrase, is *servicing a client*. What does that involve?

You've got to keep talking to your customer in bad times. It's easy to call a client up when times are really good, but you've got to be able to service a customer when times aren't good—when they're going through difficult periods. That's when they need your help the most. Service to me also means keeping your customer informed immediately about positions that they have on, any trades or executions that they make, the status of the equity in their accounts when requested. *If the customer has something in his confirmations that's going to be corrected the next day, call him ahead of time and let him know that there was a price change and that it's going to be corrected the next day—before he discovers the error!* Keep them informed of changes in their positions. I think we need to operate under the assumption that the customer wants to know of anything material in his account, and that means fills reported promptly, margin calls being sent. *The biggest problem with a lot of brokers is they won't get on the phone and call a customer about a margin call.* They think it will go away. You're better off if you get on the phone and immediately ask for the money. Number one, he'll probably satisfy the margin requirement right away, or number two, it gives you the opportunity to involve the customer in a proactive position. Maybe he ought to be getting out of the position, or maybe he ought to be doing something else.

The next word is *honesty*.

That goes without saying. We know that people, by and large, are suspicious of this business. So we have to gain their trust.

How do you gain someone's trust?

You've got to let them know who you are. For example, if you're a broker representing a particular clearing firm, you've got to let them know how it works, simple as it may seem. "Here's the way it works. You send us the money. We take the money and deposit it in a segregated account. The firm that we clear this business with is so and so," or "We're a clearing member," and you explain what that means. You explain how the business works. You need to explain the financial safeguards built into the system. The National Futures Association (NFA) has a good booklet on this: *The Financial Integrity of U.S. Futures Markets*. (Call 1-800-621-3570 or (312) 781-1300 for a free copy.)

How else do you get someone to trust you?

Well, that takes time, and it's a relationship builder. You need to impress upon them you're in this business for the long pull and a single transaction is not what you're interested in—and that your success is ultimately dependent on their success and their interests. You don't get people's trust just by showing up. You earn their trust by talking to them and listening to them during the course of the relationship. The trust process is a continuous one. *I find that for myself, even if I've had clients for years, they'll leave in a minute if they have an iota of a reason to believe that*

I'm not interested in them or that I've violated that trust even a little. Clients, consumers are sophisticated—they know they've got alternatives. They have to be assured continually, over and over, how it works. Where the money goes, how the statement reads, "Do you understand it? Any questions? Any concerns? How are you doing? How are we doing? How can we meet your needs better?"

How would you advise young brokers to polish their sales skills?

Just practice. You, first and foremost, cannot take the attitude you're not a salesman. You have to come to grips with the fact that you're paid in commissions, you're paid for doing business with people where they have an alternative—and nothing happens until something is sold. So if you go in there with the idea you've got the solution but you don't have to gain their confidence, nothing will happen. You've got to underscore the importance of sales skills first. Then you can proceed.

Any personal philosophy about this business?

I operate under a credo that's held me in good stead for a long time, and that is that the day you stop soliciting for new business is the day your business begins to die. Too many people operate under the assumption that, "I'll be a salesman for a year-and-a-half, I'll have a bunch of clients, and then I'll stop; then it's all over with and I can sit back and rake in the money." It's never that way. You have to be continuing your education, self-directed if you will, but you need to constantly have that attitude every single day. The markets are constantly moving, constantly changing. Your clients are being contacted by different brokers. You need to be on the cutting edge. This is a moving, changing business. *If you're not moving forward, you're going backwards.*

How do you stay knowledgeable?

I'm a big reader of trade publications. I read every night at home. I read about twenty newspapers a week. I get *The Wall Street Journal*, I get the *Financial Times* for the weekend. I get *Barron's*, I get *Forbes*. I retain outside research services. I try to look at who's successful in a certain commodity group: a grower, a producer, and what is it he's doing, and then try to learn as much about his business as possible. You don't see anyone who's very successful in any particular field not plugged in to the information age today.

If you had to start over again, what would you do differently, and also, what do you wish you had known when you started in this business?

Well, keep in mind that we're talking about a long time ago, over twenty years. Things are different today. I guess I would've spent a little more time with face-to-face interviews early on. As for the second part of your question, you absolutely need to value your time and be organized. I would say if I had to start over again, I think that a great piece of advice would be to focus on things that you can control and try not to put yourself into a position where you are spread too thin. Simplify your business so you stay at the cutting edge and you can operate on all cylinders. A lot of people try to do too many things. Number one, you have to value time and you have to develop a system of keeping records of whom you've contacted and what the next step is. You must keep the sales process moving toward the order. You need to constantly hold yourself up—and no one ever told me this either, but it's a little trick I always did when I was first in the business. I was constantly concerned about making a living. So every single day I kept track of the amount of business I did when I was in those early years and I knew exactly where I was. It put me on a schedule. I wish I had been told that from day one. It turns out I did it on my own. I think another piece of advice is, learn how to refuse business.

Talk about refusing business, please.

The real quagmire for a lot of brokers is that they compromise themselves by doing business with people who make them feel badly. Not only are they often credit risks, but there are other factors. You need to be willing to say "no" to types of relationships based on hunches, and that's not necessarily being an élitist. It means you that know some of us get along with certain people better than others. Probably one of my biggest mistakes over the years has been that I've been on kind of a mission at times, saying, "I'm bound and determined to win this prospect over." No matter what you did, it would not make any difference. You could be walking on water and he'd say, "Yeah, but your feet are wet." The bottom line is, you need to realize there are certain kinds of people who aren't going to be pleased, ever. When you run across somebody who's rejecting you so resoundingly, don't keep the prospect or lead on the mantle like a china egg; toss it. Don't look at it anymore. Go on to the next prospect, there are just too many fish in the sea.

Anything else about refusing business?

Yes, even if it's your biggest and best customer, you may someday have to refuse his trades. The customer's trading, not because he likes you, but because he's trying to make money. What I sense is a lot of brokers fall in love with the client, fall in love with the action of, "We're making lots of money." You should never let a single customer become so important that he can ruin your business—and that's very easy to have happen. You have to be more on top of a clients' qualifications. Whenever the customer begins trading significantly, and gives even the slightest hint of not being qualified, you need to take the bull by the horns and, for lack of anything else, either insist that he liquidate or send in more money—as soon as possible. And if he doesn't like it, he can transfer his positions to another house. It can happen with accelerated rates of trading that if that customer blows up in your face, you're going to have a problem and your business will be gone. You need to take major steps to almost withdraw from that type of relationship or get him under control because you're going to lose the client anyway.

How do you keep a client from being a plunger?

Tell them the truth. Tell them how much money we're talking about. Go over the numbers. Tell them exactly what it means—that gets their attention. Do the arithmetic. It's the truth serum.

Doug, anything you want to say in closing?

Too often I think our business is looked at as a quick fix, quick easy money, when in fact it's the hardest way in the world to make a buck. But this is a wonderful business. I'm glad it's here. I don't have many regrets. It's been a good career for me. I plan to stay in it for the rest of my life.

Hartley Connett

Chemical Bank
New York, New York

Would you please tell us something about yourself, Hartley?

I grew up in the Philadelphia area, and as a kid I visited my grand-parents in New York a lot. I really liked the City and vowed when I was very young that I would work there someday. I didn't know what I wanted to do, but I knew I wanted to make it in New York. I played lots of sports all through grade school, high school, and college, mostly baseball and basketball. Some people say I'm rather competitive (big smile). I do know I hate to lose, so I guess I am competitive. I think you'll find a lot of people in this business who are very competitive, who tended to be more active in athletics when they were younger, whatever sport it might have been, and carried that with them into the commodities area. Just look at the business itself. You look at what happens even on the floor, the competition there, the pushing and shoving and establishing of space and keeping that space: I think it all sort of fits.

Do you think you need to be competitive to do your job?

I think it's important from the brokering standpoint, from the sales and marketing standpoint. You have to be able to accept rejection a lot and pick yourself up from the floor when you don't get the sale or the orders you'd like to be getting. That's an important quality I think you do have to have to be successful as a broker in this business.

Any early jobs that prepared you for the futures business?

My first real job was with a company that sold engineering graphics equipment.

What year was this?

1979. My first sales territory was Lower Manhattan. If you can, imagine a young kid coming from the suburbs of Philadelphia for his first time being thrown out onto the streets of Lower Manhattan, making cold calls on people to sell them various drawing materials and graphic design packages. It was tough, but I learned a lot, especially about selling.

What did you learn about selling?

It toughened me up. It gets back to that whole rejection thing. I would literally be thrown out of people's offices—"And don't ever call on me again!"—that type of thing. If that happened three or four times, and one time you got somebody who said, "Yeah, I am interested actually, that looks pretty good, let's talk," you would very quickly forget all the other times that didn't go so well.

In late 1980, I got a call from a commodity broker friend of mine. He called to tell me there was something interesting going on in the commodity markets—they had just introduced a heating-oil contract. I wasn't quite sure what he was talking about. He said a big part of this job was sales and marketing. "You've been successful at selling what you're doing now, and this could be a really good opportunity." So he gave me the name of this guy who worked for E. F. Hutton. Hutton at the time was one of the first companies to establish a national petroleum desk to service commercial oil companies that would be using the newly-introduced heating-oil futures contract. That was important to me. This was an opportunity to get in on the ground floor on a desk that was really gearing itself up to be a commercial player on the brokerage side of this business. I remember going in and meeting with this gentleman who had been recruited by E. F. Hutton from a major oil company. He was talking to me about wet barrels and paper barrels and I didn't have a clue as to what he was talking about, but it sounded interesting so I signed on. My first job was basically sitting in the middle of a horseshoe-shaped desk where brokers threw pieces of paper at me and I phoned those orders down to the floor of the exchange, reported back the executions, updated the status of each order, reported partial fills, anything and everything having to do with the orders. I did that for about two months or so.

Then what?

Then I was moved to the desk and given a few smaller accounts to start talking with on a regular basis. Some of the accounts our desk handled were big commercial players. Back then there were very few people who were providing brokerage services, so I really got a lot of good exposure to a lot of companies. I worked hard to learn how the markets functioned. It certainly did help that I had a mentor who knew quite a bit about the cash-oil business. While we talked a lot about the technical side of the market and the commodity side, it's helped me to be able to understand and to talk the language that refiners and producers speak every day. *Regardless of* what market you're specializing in, it is very important for any broker to *understand that market.* Go visit the producers or processors or farmers or ranchers. Learn their business. The technical side of the market is obviously very important, and it's part of the market my clients are most interested in getting from me as a broker. These clients usually know the fundamentals, the broker supplies technical information mostly, but you must have the ability to speak the fundamental language of the industry you're communicating with. This really helps you establish yourself as a credible broker with the people you service. You may as well be aware of this. You've got to be more knowledgeable than the brokers you're competing with, and that takes work.

Now, you had a mentor. Some people reading this chapter aren't going to have mentors, but they're going to be interested in specializing. How would they get up to speed? How would they learn an industry?

Well, you can find information on any industry if you're willing to look. There are books available. Read the appropriate trade journals. Seek out the people you're trying to do business with. If you're trying to learn the business, nobody has a problem sitting down and teaching you about it, or at the very least recommending books, videos, classes, even field visits and plant tours. A lot of clients rely on me for certain technical information and what's happening on the floor in my part of the business. So they have absolutely no problem if I want to sit down with them and say, "Hey, teach me something here. Do you have an hour?" or whatever. They love to talk about their industry, and I think it makes for a much better client-broker relationship. Don't be afraid to ask. Don't be afraid to say, "Hey, I'm going to be in town. Can I get you for lunch or dinner? I want to learn a little more about this part of the business." I've never found a problem doing that.

So you're handling these little accounts, and they trust you now to do some of that. So now how does your career progress? That's 1980.

I took a great deal of interest in what I was doing, in really learning the industry. I mean, *I was coming in at four, sometimes five, never later, in the morning because we were trading the London market as well.* I put in a lot of hours. I was the new guy on the block. I didn't mind doing that.

So you came to work at four o'clock.

Yes, I would always be there about when the London markets opened. We had plenty of U.S.-based clients who were actively trading the London market, too, so there was a lot of arbitrage activity. It took a lot of work and time to understand the business. Eventually, the more senior people who were running the department started giving me exposure to some of the larger accounts.

How did you expand your business?

There was a lot of cold calling involved. I just made a lot of calls. We had a pretty good grasp of the fundamental side of the business and we were able to show these companies how they might be able to benefit from futures. We gave them charts, did regression analysis, anything and everything to help them.

And you did this even if they weren't clients?

Oh yes, absolutely. At some point you make a decision as to how much time you are going to spend on a prospect. As we were developing our business, it wasn't a requirement for the prospect to sign account forms for us to be talking to him. There have been times when I've worked for two or three years to develop a relationship with a prospect until I actually got to the point where account papers were signed. You don't want too many of those kinds of prospects because they are a lot of work. You target ones who are so big that you're going to put the time in. We also developed daily commentary reports which we sent out to people. This was a good prospecting and sales tool. Providing somebody with a fax each night and showing them the high, low, and settlement prices, with a short, technical commentary, was valuable to a lot of people. Some of them didn't even have screens back then.

When you made your cold calls, did you just talk to people on the phone, or did you go out to see people as well?

Both. Normally, I would say it starts with the phone. You've got to pick the phone up, you've got to know the right person to get to, make your pitch over the phone first, and establish yourself. That's not always easy. Cold calling isn't an easy thing.

How do you find the key person at a company to talk to?

Well, for us it was pretty easy. Most of the oil companies were segmented so you knew where the actual trading department was. Whoever was actually trading the physical crude oil or gasoline was more than likely the person who was executing the futures contracts. Some companies did their futures trading in the treasury area, so you might speak to a different person. There are, in any company, people who are responsible for trading, who are actually pulling the trigger every day on the trades. Then there are people who are responsible for selecting the brokerage house they're going to do business with. In many cases that may be the same person; in other cases it's not. If it's the trader, the one pulling the trigger on the trades, obviously you need to have a relationship with him. If the CFO (Chief Financial Officer) or the treasurer is the guy who makes the decisions, you'd better have a relationship with him as well. So I think, as a salesman, you need to establish, "Who are the decision makers here? Where do I have to have my relationships?" They may be on different levels or in different departments. Obviously, on the trader's side, he's going to be most interested in your execution capabilities, your information, "Can you help me figure this thing out?" On the treasurer's level, obviously the comfort of your firm's balance sheet, and the name and history of the company are going to be important.

Hartley, have you ever taken any sales classes?

Yes, I did, as part of my training for the first job I had in New York. We had a two-week sales school in Chicago, where the home office was. That was very helpful. It was run by senior sales people in the company and that exercise was very important.

Can you remember what you learned? What sales advice do you have?

I think the most important thing is that you have to be a good listener. I really think that's the key. I think you can look real snazzy, you can have a great presentation, that's all well and good, but that may not be what that particular customer is looking for. So I think listening is really the key to being able to find out and understand that particular client's needs, and then to being able to respond to them. *I think you'll find that the most successful brokers are those who are customer-oriented, who have listened to their clients say, "This is really what we need."* It may vary from client to client, but that's the key. When you listen, really listen, you are able to provide that customer with a customer-oriented product.

How do you get people to open up so you have an opportunity to listen?

That gets back to having an understanding of the fundamental side of the business. I've found that people will open up with me more if they feel comfortable that I have a good knowledge of their business. We talk a little about what's happening in the physical oil market. I think they realize I can relate to them on that level, but they understand I'm not an expert. I haven't spent any time *working* in the oil industry, but I've spent the time *learning* about it. That gets back to having a knowledge of the industry you want to service.

Did you do any spec business then, or has yours always been hedge business?

Purely commercial business. We don't do any retail spec business at all. It is one hundred percent oil trade business, which includes major oil companies, producers, refiners, and end-users; people who are in the physical market every single day.

Do you ask for referrals?

Early on in my career, no, I didn't. That was one of the things I probably should have done earlier. Brokers should always ask for referrals, but not be a pest about it. If you've got a good relationship with a client, you don't always have to ask, but you should ask once in a while—particularly when things are really going well with that particular client. Some brokers are too proud to ask, but I really think clients like to help you. It ties them closer to you. When you do someone a favor, doesn't it tie you closer to them?

Any advice about servicing an account?

You have to stay focused. It gets back to the whole listening point. You've got to get to know as much as you're allowed to know about your customer. You have to relate on the trading level. Our clients have to know they can call us, our phones aren't going to be busy, we can get them right to the floor, the execution is consistent every day. When market news breaks, we call them right away. Our operations people also must relate well to the operations people at the oil companies—that all has to run smoothly every day, too. If treasury isn't happy with the back office function, you can lose that account just as easily as if you did something wrong on the trading side. So you have to be focused in that area. We send our operations people out to meet with their operations people.

Everybody does it differently, so you've got to be responsive to your clients' back office administrative people. I think everybody tries to make this business a lot more glamorous than it really is. A lot of it is doing the simple things correctly, and on time.

How do you handle the pressure and the stress?

Well, I smoke a lot. Of course, that's not the way to do it. You've got to be healthy, you've got to be active. When you leave the trading desk, leave the business behind you. Go home, enjoy your life, your family, play basketball, run, whatever you do, but relieve the stress in as healthful a way as you can. This business: socializing, taking clients out to dinner, doing what you have to, occasionally the late nights—I don't see how you can avoid that at the broker level, but don't make a habit of it. It catches up with you very quickly. If you're not careful, it can take its toll. You must stay sharp to do your job. Every time I enter an order onto the floor, I've got a risk there. I've got credit risk every day. I've got to report back accurately to the clients what they've actually done . . . or we may have problems. The phones are ringing constantly. You've got to realize that stress is part of the job. I think being active is important, whatever it is you're into, do it and be on a regular regime. Keep yourself as healthy as possible.

You do your best and that's it. If you're worried about every time a client told you that you gave them a lousy fill, or said, "That was a pretty lousy call you made on the market," you'll never come back. Another thing, understand your own capabilities and limitations. Clients appreciate that.

Any advice to young brokers about prospecting?

What's worked well for me, personally, is targeting. Target who you want to prospect. Focus. For me, what has always worked best is to target the people who I feel are the most desirable clients, the ones I want to have a relationship with. It may not be the biggest company or it may not be a company or even industry that is currently using the futures markets, but soon they might be. They *should* be.

I do my homework in terms of whom I want to target. I learn as much as I can about that company so I can start talking their language, so I can start talking about the aspects of the market that relate to their business. *I target the prospects I want to go after, and then I go after them with a vengeance. "These are my five prospects that I'm going to work on really hard for the next month." It's important that you give yourself a time-frame so you don't drag it out with a particular company, or spin your wheels.*

How do people know how long to prospect? How do they know if they are spinning their wheels?

Well, as difficult as it may be sometimes, I think that you have to ask questions of the prospect: "How am I doing? Where do you stand now? Has the information been good? Are you getting close to deciding about an account? Are you reviewing any relationships?" You have to ask them.

A minute ago you said you prospect with a vengeance. What are some of your prospecting tools?

I focus on what I think is important. For instance, I might do a special write-up I see in the market that only applies to them. Now, it takes me time to do that. I do it after market hours. I go to the computer and I write up an interesting, special situation, oriented to a specific risk they might have. I'll send that kind of material to them. We have broad, general, market commentaries that are easy to send, but that's what everyone else does who's trying to get their business. I like to do special write-ups for them.

Anything else you do when you're barraging a prospect?

Well, if I get to know that this guy likes fishing or something, I might send him a little fishing article. Again, that's all part of getting to know your prospect. Know the trader's personality, what he likes. A little article on fly-fishing, if that's what he's into, might be neat. Maybe send him a book. I don't know, but things like that. On the business side, as I mentioned, I prepare special situation reports tailored to their problems, their needs.

*I draw from the equity research reports our company
does. I think any broker working for a large firm should access
this information. Certainly there's an equity research person who's
probably focusing on a particular industry or company that the
broker may be prospecting.* Now if my company feels very posi-
tively about an oil producer I'm prospecting, I use that as a lead-
in. I say, "Oh, by the way, you might want to know that my
company is rating your stock as a buy right now." You can use
that. It won't work in every case, but I'll certainly use it if I see
that it fits in with what I'm trying to do. *Use the resources in
your company.*

Can you give us an example about prospecting?

I go back to one specific presentation I can remember giving years
ago to a group of senior oil executives from a company that was
going out for the first time, expecting to get into the futures market. They were going to evaluate a number of different futures
brokers and then decide who to go with. After we'd gone through
our general "Here's who we are, here's the company," and all
that, I remember one of the people getting up and asking me the
question, "What sort of things can you do for us?" My response
to it was, "What do you want us to do? What is important to
you? What sort of things do you need help in? We're good at
doing a lot of things, I could go through a whole list of things, but
it may not mean anything to you. What are your needs?" I was
told several weeks later, when I went back down to Houston and
revisited them, that the one thing that impressed them the most
was that response: "What do you want us to do for you?"

Hartley, how does honesty fit in to all of this?

Honesty is the most important thing, especially in this business. I
don't know if our industry gets any more bad press than any other

industry, but it certainly seems the press is always angling in on the worst aspects of our business. There are bad apples in any business.

What does honesty mean in the way you do your business?

I'm not here to trade the markets. I'm here to provide a service, and I get paid for providing that service well and consistently every day. You don't ever break the rules, but there are times when there are a lot of gray areas. For example, if you have a client who wants to buy at a certain price level. Let's say it's $18.00 crude. He's been trying to buy there and it's touching there and touching there and he's not getting filled. So he puts in an $18.01 bid, and we get fast market conditions and it trades $18.00. It trades through him, and the market starts going up and he's still not filled, and he's saying, "Well, you owe me a fill." Well, you don't owe the customer a fill. Your obligation is to do the best job you can, using due diligence to try to get that customer filled. He's not entitled to a fill, and you can make a mistake there. If every time that happens, at whatever level you eventually ended up filling him, you adjust him back down to the $18.00, $18.01 level, you can cause yourself problems. I think you can get in the habit of doing that. The customer all of a sudden starts to expect that just because you're not getting things filled at his price that you're going to adjust his price, and he's not happy when you can't do that. *So honesty to me is playing by the rules.* You understand it's an open outcry system, and it's not perfect, but it's still the most efficient system we have. You play within the rules and you provide good, honest, fair, consistent service. Our business is no different from any other business. There are a lot of opportunities to circumvent the rules. That's why it's important that you explain to the customer how it works. You've got to spend time educating customers about how things work on the floor. You have to explain about fast markets, slippage, all of that. Sure, you explain time and sales, too. *Educate the clients so they know exactly why they're not always going to get filled at their price.*

Do you work at home?

Sometimes I will call London from home to see what's going on, but I don't do that as much as I used to. I mean, if there's anything going on overnight, I can get calls at any time, or if there's news breaking, people will call.

What do you mean, anytime?

Anytime from three in the morning until ten at night, somebody could call me. It could be a client sitting and watching a news show down in San Antonio who says, "Hey, I just saw this, what do you think?" It could be London calling and saying, "We have some news breaking in the market, you might want to let some of your clients know." We can cut down on those types of calls, though, because we now have the ACCESS trading system, which trades through the night—all of our clients have direct access to ACCESS. If there's been some news flying around, if the market's been volatile, as I said, I might call from home to check and see what the overseas markets are doing. I do have a portable phone that's on most of the time, so if I'm on the train or something, or if I'm travelling, prospecting, I can always be reached.

What's your day like?

I usually catch the 7:01 express, get to Grand Central in about thirty minutes, and then walk about five minutes to work. We have faxes that have come in from London, so I read those right away. Read all the news headlines and reports that came in over-night on the screens. Then I just start calling the customers. We establish what the opening call is going to be based on what happened in London overnight or what ACCESS trading might have done, and then just start finding out what's going on in the market. You get a lot of information just from talking to clients. "What did you hear?" "Well, I've heard this, you heard that." I talk to cash brokers to get an idea of what the physical market is doing. Just basically try to get as much information as you can.

We have also established some pretty good relationships with the news services, the people who put the headlines up, so occasionally we'll get a call as a headline comes out. "Just want you to know that. . . ." We don't ever like our clients to trade off of headlines. That isn't the right way to do things, but it's nice to know that if something comes out and breaks, we'll often find out right away. So we do develop relationships with the press, to make sure we're wired into what's going on.

From there you have to be prepared for whatever might break in the market. As I mentioned earlier, during lulls you want to find the time to call the prospects you're working on. I think that it's important to call them with good information, and I like to keep it short. No rumors—don't do that. Try to give prospects something that you're pretty certain they're not getting from somebody else. You have to find the time to do that. If there's nothing going on, I have a little spiel. I call a client or a prospect up and say, "Hey, just wanted to give you a noon update here. Market's pretty quiet, forty thousand lots have traded, really haven't seen too much here; if we see anything really good we'll give you a call." That kind of thing. You want to do that regularly. I mean, some days you can't. Some days you can't—you're just wired into your clients, they're so active you just have to stay with them.

Do you go to lunch?

We have lunches ordered up and delivered here at the desk. Now, certainly if a client's in town, we'll go out and have a lunch with a client or we'll hit the road and have lunch with prospects, but the normal day is coming in the morning and being attached to the desk most of the day.

After the markets close, what happens from then until the time you go home?

Well, that's when the roll-up-the-sleeves grunt work starts. We have trades to process. We have a lot of confirmation reports that go out to the clients on all the trades they did that day. We've got to check out with the floor brokers, and then we've got our check-out procedure and all our administrative stuff. You're trying to catch any mistakes. Very important to check out with your executing brokers to confirm everything they reported, just to double, triple check. I like to call all the clients and give 'em a recap. Afternoon is not a bad time to call prospects, either. After the market closes and people settle down, you can do some of your prospecting.

You've seen several brokers during your career. What are some traits of successful brokers?

Well, I think without exception, the ones who are successful year in and year out are the ones who are really into the industry, who are in the market constantly. They enjoy the market, they enjoy the activity. You have to be able to talk the market, and you're not going to do that if you don't have a real enthusiasm for the way the market behaves and what drives it.

You're learning new things every day. I've been in the business more than fifteen years and I'm still learning, every day. There's always something to learn.

*I would say that calling the market right every day is one thing you **don't** have to be so concerned about.* You don't have a crystal ball. You've got a conviction, an idea: back it up fundamentally and technically. Okay, if it gets here and you're wrong, you're out. Clients will never have a problem with that. The problem is the brokers who are saying, "You've got to buy it, you've got to buy it, it's going up." There are a lot of guys I've seen who've done that. They'll get that one good run, but the law of averages always catches up to them. Don't be a real aggressive "gotta buy, gotta sell" man. Don't try to be the hero who's going to outguess the market. You've got to be flexible. Give them all the information you've got. "Based on that information, it's my opinion that this is what might happen. On the other hand. . . ." I mean, you have to hedge yourself a little bit. *They want to know your opinion, but make sure it's based on good reasons.*

Be humble. Be careful about how you talk the market. Talk intelligently. Know what you're talking about. Do as much research, homework, talk to as many people as you can, get a feel for what's going on fundamentally. If you do recommend something, say, "I feel it's going to do this because of these fundamental reasons and these technical reasons. If this happens and it gets over this level, I'm out." Establish what your risk and reward parameters are. Be professional.

Brokers from the seventies and eighties. What advice do you have for those brokers who were once successful but are now floundering?

Well, there may be any number of reasons why this happens. I think you have to first take stock of yourself. Go off, sit down and try to figure out what's happened to you. It could be any number of things. Markets have changed a lot in the nineties. New technology, new terminology, computer eggheads everywhere. I've been up against that. I don't think it's so difficult to deal with, but you've got to be on top of it. You've got to spend as much time with those people as possible. Ultimately, I think it's a pretty simple business. You are trying to buy low and sell high; I don't care how complicated or sophisticated you want to make it. That's the name of the game, but all this new stuff may be the reason for your difficulty. If that's the case, you need to learn more about what's happening in the newer market.

There are a lot of electronic advances happening now. We all need to start thinking now about how to position ourselves to either capture these opportunities, or change the way we're doing business now because of them. The commodity business in the eighties was a whole lot different from the commodity business in the nineties. There are a lot more people involved now, the markets are a lot more efficient, there are a lot more instruments, there's a whole new group of people. Younger people, very smart people, have come in who are doing different things from what the guys in the eighties were doing. Yet, I don't think that a good broker who is keeping up and who is in the market and asking all the right questions is ever going to be obsolete. Don't be intimidated. You know about the market: what's moving these markets around is supply and demand, and that's happening today, it was happening in the eighties, it was happening in the 1800s! That hasn't changed. That'll never change, but I think some people have gotten frightened off and haven't developed relationships with the new types of traders out there because they've been a little intimidated by them.

I've heard people say this is a relationship business. Do you agree with that?

Yes. At the end of the day, I think somebody does business with a broker because he likes you, he trusts you, he thinks you're honest. You've got to do a good job for him, of course. He feels comfortable with you, and he knows if there's a problem, you're going to do everything you can to take care of it. You're going to look after his best interests. Getting back to the successful versus the not-so-successful brokers, the difference is that successful brokers get to know their clients. I mean, I've got some great friendships with customers that will never go away, even if they stop doing business.

Can you think of a mistake or two that you have made that other brokers can learn from? Or any successes they could learn from?

There are a lot. On both sides. Well, to me, if there was a mistake it would have been during a period when I had moved a little bit too far away from the customers and lost touch with some of them. I think if you're going to be a broker, you are going to go through those periods where you're up and then you're down and then you've got to build back up again. You're going to lose customers, something's going to happen and it's going to be totally out of your control. Right there, there's a lesson: be as diverse as you can in terms of your client base. In my business, you don't want to service just the users. You want to service the users *and* producers. And you want as many of the people in between as you can get because there are going to be times in any market when it will be far more advantageous for a producer to do something that it would be for a user.

Another mistake people make is they get one account, and it's just a huge account, and they really don't develop any other business. They get to the point where eighty percent of their business is coming from this one account or this closely related group of accounts. I've made that mistake myself. I corrected it, but if you're looking at your monthly P & L sheet or your customer-activity sheets, and you see that, for a couple months running, one client is thirty-five or forty percent of your business, red flags should go up.

Any war stories?

Well, I don't know if you'd call this a war story, but I'd been prospecting this big company for close to a year. I knew they only had one other relationship, so that fit the criteria for me. They had only one broker. It was a solid relationship. I got my foot in the door. I started to make a dent, and I started to click with this guy, the head trader, and we were getting along very well personally. I thought I was really getting close, and he called me up and said, "Hartley, I'm coming into New York, and I want to see you. We'll get together." I'm feeling really good because this guy's coming to New York just to see me. This is nothing but good news, this is great. We'd just recently had a little golf outing and that went beautifully. So he comes to New York, and we meet. *I'm all ready to start talking about account papers, and we go out to lunch, and he proceeds to tell me, "I've done some analyzing and everything else, and I need to tell you that I can't open the account right now. You haven't given me enough reasons yet to justify going to the board to get this account opened." I said, "You're kidding me." I threw him off guard there. I was just so shocked; I couldn't believe it. He said, "No." So I said, "Well, okay, I'm obviously shocked, but let's proceed to have a nice lunch" which we did, and we chatted. So anyway, he went back and I was trying to think of all the reasons why this happened. Our price was certainly competitive. Our service had been excellent. During the recent three months there had been a lot of things going on in the market where we were getting news for him that he wasn't getting from his other brokers. We just had a wonderful golf outing in a very nice professional setting. I just couldn't think of what the problem was. So I wrote everything down in a letter to him saying, "Thank you for being honest with me, I understand where you're coming from, but I really think there are a number of reasons here why you ought to reconsider this." I wrote them all down, point by point. I finished it up by saying, "Given the above, I don't see any reason why you wouldn't open the account with me now. If there is a reason you can give me"— because he really wasn't specific—"then please let me know." The letter went out and three days later I got a phone call and it was, "Hartley, I've reconsidered, you're right. We're going to open an account with you. Send me the papers."*

Now, there wasn't anything magical about that letter, but I think, obviously the theme here is, don't give up. Don't ever give up. I think you can tell when it's a lost cause, you can tell that, but I knew that it wasn't over. There was something here, something just a little bit more that I needed to push him over, and it was nothing more than just a letter. You may be down by twenty points in the fourth quarter, but man, you can still come back. Especially when you've really invested the time and you know that you've done a good job with the prospect. Don't be afraid to just pinpoint. "What is it? What am I doing wrong here?" Don't give up.

Marvelous story. I just have a couple of final questions. If you had three pieces of advice to young brokers, what would they be?

One: know your customers, so you can provide them with customer-oriented service. Find out their needs and fill them if you can. If you can't, don't pretend.

Two: know your market. Learn as much as you possibly can. This is an ongoing experience. It gets back to what I think separates the good brokers from the bad brokers. It can't be a part-time thing. You can't just watch the screens and pay attention to what's going on and just call somebody and say, "Hey, how're you doing?" You've got to have something to give them every time you call. Be aware of what's happening on the exchanges. Are there new rules? Are there new contracts? Are there new specifications? A lot of times customers are unaware of simple announcements by exchanges or how contracts might be changing.

Three: don't let the stress get to you. You've got to walk away from it. You've got to stay physically fit, physically active. Understand that a lot of selling goes into this job, just like any other sales job, but unlike many other sales jobs, there's a lot that can go wrong during the day. You obviously have to deal with those problems, but don't take them home with you. Pick it up fresh the next day.

Are there any books, tapes, courses you could recommend?

I have a box of *Reminiscences of a Stock Operator* by Jesse Livermore at home, and that's a book I still give to new prospects. I mean, everybody treats that as the one book every commodity broker should have in his or her briefcase. These kinds of books can be very helpful when you have a new trader coming in and you want to give him a little bit of a feel for the business.

If you want a basic book that pretty much covers all that you hear about in terms of technical analysis, John Murphy's book on Technical Analysis is good.

Anything else?

Well, I would say to anyone who is looking to get into this, there are no guarantees in this business at all. This is not the most secure business to get into, so you have to be entrepreneurial and independent to begin with. If you don't think you're that kind of person, you think it's going to be easy, and you're going to make a lot of money as a commodity broker without a lot of work, forget about it. People make this business out to be a lot more glamorous than it really is. You've heard all the stories, but for every success story, there is a failure. I think you need to recognize that going in. I don't think there is any blueprint for success. It's tough, it's challenging, but the rewards can be pretty tremendous if you do things right. It certainly isn't just doing what *I* say. There are many successful brokers in this business we all can learn from.

Robert T. Conrardy

Cargill Investor Services
Chicago, Illinois

Bob, please tell us a little bit about yourself and how you got into this business.

I've always been interested in the area of finance and banking. I guess that is why I decided to major in it as an undergrad at the University of Wisconsin and later as a graduate student at the University of Chicago. My first job was as a financial planner with a small outfit in Madison, Wisconsin. I came to Chicago and started here at Cargill Investor Services (CIS) about ten years ago as a management trainee. I started in the S&P pit at the Chicago Merc.

Bob, is sales important in your job? Is the ability to sell important for a broker to succeed in this business?

The ability to communicate your ideas, to work as a partner with your client, to consult with your client is very important. Whether you consider that sales, I don't know. Your client should not feel that you're using "sales techniques" to try and sell him something.

But if a broker said to you, "What does it mean to be a good salesman? What do I have to do to be a good salesman?" what would you say to him or her?

I would say there are a couple things you need to do to become a good salesman. First, you need to have a high level of integrity with your clients. A good example of this is the broker's ability to handle orders so the client knows he's getting fair and equitable fills.

How would a client know if he got a fair and equitable fill?

Most clients, especially the institutional ones, will be watching the markets and they'll understand if a fill they received was not done in a timely or accurate manner or wasn't done effectively.

So they have screens in their offices, and they put the order in with you, but if you took a couple extra minutes to get the order to the pit they would know that, and the market's taking off in the meantime. That kind of thing?

Yes, that's one way of showing your professionalism and diligence in handling their business. Other ways include working with the clients to meet their needs. I deal with institutional clients: money center banks, mutual funds, pension funds, and other money managers.   We work hard to make sure we're doing a good job.

How do you find out how you're doing with a client?

Well, the first thing to do is ask. We've put together structured questionnaires we've used with a number of clients. We ask the client how we've done over the last six months, year, whatever. Have we shown any improvement? Have our services gotten worse or better? If we're doing things well, what are we doing well? If we're doing things poorly, what are we doing poorly? Who else in the industry is doing as good a job or better? We're trying to benchmark ourselves against the other people in the industry. What are my competitors doing that we should do to meet clients' needs better?

How did the CIS part of your career happen?

Well, I knew that I was planning on going to Chicago because it offered a lot of opportunities in the financial and banking markets, and I used the University of Wisconsin School of Business placement office. I noticed an ad in one of their alumni newsletters saying that Cargill Investor Services was looking for a management trainee.

Any advice to young brokers about prospecting?

The key thing is to pick a market in which to specialize. Do they want to deal with institutional clients or retail clients? Within those categories you also need to target. You can't be a jack of all trades; you can't be everything to everyone. Once you've established your area of specialization, that's when you say to yourself, okay, who should I be targeting? When I came into this business, I knew I wanted to target institutional clients.

But do you just go knock on some bank's door? How do you do all that?

You can network and meet people. One way is to go to some conferences in your industry or become active in industry groups. For example, at an exchange, I was an advisor to the stock index futures committee. Committees are always looking for advice and input. It's also a good way to learn more about the industry and get some experience, if you're sincere and willing to work. In addition, it's a great way to meet people.

How did you get picked for that?

I submitted my name and asked people to sponsor me to be an advisor. I've also taken part in some Chicago Board of Trade research seminars. They're attended by professors as well as research people from different firms in the industry. These seminars can be very useful. You not only get to meet people, but it's a great way to increase your knowledge.

How about a broker in Lincoln, Nebraska or Pittsburgh, Pennsylvania? Suppose he's already decided on his niche. Then what does he do?

Well, I can only tell you what I do, what works for me. I target people who are already using the product. I don't go after someone who doesn't use the product because there's just too much of a learning curve to overcome. From there, I begin to prospect them, telling them about CIS and myself, as well as, how we can provide beneficial services to them. Mostly we talk about their needs and concerns. Overall, we try to match those needs with our benefits and provide good service.

What does this mean, to provide good service? What constitutes good service?

Good service consists of a number of things. One, being very responsive to the customer. Providing accurate and timely information to them. Being very dependable. They can depend on your being there, and if not you, then one of your colleagues. Our desk consists of a team, not a bunch of individual/independent brokers. It's also important to be personable. In this industry, people tend to do business with people they like.

But if a typical broker says, "How do I get people to like to do business with me?" is there an answer to that question?

I guess not everyone is going to like everybody, and that's one thing you have to understand from the beginning. What you have to do when talking with clients is to find out what their interests are. If those interests are very similar to yours, right away you probably know there is something you have in common, and usually things will click.

You mean like fishing or golf or those kinds of interests?

It could be outside of work, but I think the interest could be the markets themselves; for example, if you're covering fixed income markets and your prospects or clients are in these markets, you have a common interest and there's something to talk about. Sure, outside interests can give you something to talk about, too, and that can help to strengthen a relationship.

Okay, back to prospecting. Here is this broker in Pittsburgh and he wants to go after institutional business. So he targets

Mellon Bank. Who does he go see at Mellon Bank? "Hi, this is Jim Smith with XYZ Futures." The bank's response, "Get out of here, we already have a broker." Maybe he doesn't start with Mellon. What does that broker do?

First of all, *he needs to understand what benefits he can provide to the client.* It may sound corny, but I like to think of the benefits I can provide to my clients as my tool box. For example, in my tool box, one of the key benefits I have is my firm. I come from a very reputable firm. CIS is known for handling institutional business. It is very strongly capitalized with a very good balance sheet and is a firm where employees are not allowed to trade on behalf of their own accounts. So there's no concern about conflicts of interest, which is often important to institutional clients. I also tell them we are very good at servicing our clients' needs. There could be a number of things that a new broker may have in his so called tool box. He needs to understand how those benefits can match the prospects' needs. If the prospect is a large institution looking for a broker with a solid balance sheet and financial stability, and you have that in your tool box, that is definitely something you should use in leveraging your prospecting efforts.

But how do you even get an audience? How do you even get in to see those people?

Many times I'll call them or write a letter and follow up with a call. The most success, however, usually comes from referral business. I try to get referral business from my clients who are already using the product and who know I do a good job handling their business. This way, they're usually not afraid to give me a referral.

Do you help your clients trade? Or do they call their own shots?

It depends on the customer. Some customers use me merely for execution. They know what they need to do and at what price levels, so they just use us for execution and clearing of the trade. They may not be interested in any ideas or suggestions.

Why wouldn't those people go to the cheapest execution house they can go to?

What they're really looking for is overall service. They're looking for people who can do a very effective job executing. They're also looking for financial strength. As I mentioned earlier, when you are dealing with institutional clients, capitalization is very important. Also, they're looking for firms that have access to information, or they may be dissatisfied with the firm they're presently using.

At an opportune time I ask, "Is there anyone else I should be talking to at your firm? If you're satisfied with our information, if you're comfortable with our service, should I be talking to other people who are trading on behalf of your firm?" By doing this, I have found that business can be expanded easily through the use of referrals within the same firm. In addition to that, some of my clients eventually leave their present firm to work with another. That's another opportunity to increase one's business. Hopefully, you'll retain the business that you have at the first firm and gain some new business from the person in his new job.

Bob, how competitive does a broker have to be to succeed in this business?

I guess you have to be competitive, but I don't consider myself to be cutthroat. I don't see myself as a back stabber or anything like that. The reason I believe I have been successful at going after new business is that I have a product to offer which I think meets clients' needs. I'm very comfortable with what I'm doing. I know the markets. I feel very comfortable with my knowledge and skills with regard to the markets. Furthermore, I'm very comfortable in presenting and selling my industry, company, and products. New brokers coming into the business, first need to build this comfort level. They should do that by learning all they can about their market place, and that's not easy. It takes work. It takes time. It's impossible to sell something you know little about, or at least most people feel uncomfortable doing so.

What are some questions to ask that get people to open up?

Well, typically when talking to anyone, whether it's a prospect or a present client, if you want to find out what they're thinking, you ask an open-ended question. An open-ended question is a question that requires more than just a yes or no response. An example would be, "John, what's going on with you today?"

What are some examples of questions to get institutional prospects to open up about their business?

Ask questions regarding areas in which they have a big interest. Ask them about their jobs or their business. Everyone usually likes to tell you about their jobs or business.

So you just say, "Tell me about your business?"

It can't come off as a pat question. You need to show that you have a true interest in what they're doing, what their business is. If their business is managing money, you might ask how well they did last year—especially if you know they did okay. If their performance bombed, of course, you might ask what factors attributed to the poor performance or perhaps avoid asking them this question altogether. You might ask what their thoughts are on different money management techniques or on certain ways of managing a particular risk. You must know enough about their business to ask intelligent questions and to carry on an intelligent conversation. This includes knowing who the key people in their industry are and any current news or events. You may need to do a little bit of research in periodicals. I scan a lot of magazines for articles of interest about my industry and regarding any of my clients. If I find something, I might mention in my next conversation, "I see that *Forbes* mentioned this about you," or "I saw you in *Worth Magazine*," or "Opening up *The Wall Street Journal* today, I saw your company was mentioned on page three. If you don't have it or missed it, I'd be glad to fax you a copy of the article."

Bob, the people on your desk seemed to be in high spirits after the market closed. They seemed loose, relaxed, even happy.

You need to have a positive attitude. It gets back to what I was saying before. People like to do business with people they like. Having a positive attitude helps attract people, whether it's the people with whom you're working or people with whom you're doing business. Let's face it, sometimes this is a very tough business, and having a negative attitude can only be to your disadvantage.

Any special tips about work habits?

One of mine: do your best to be first with any news that will help your customer. Do your best to be one step ahead of him. Not for one-upsmanship, but to be helpful. To add value. Value-added, that's what I'm being paid for.

Any others tips?

One that naturally pays off is the habit of producing error-free trades, error-free paper work. Doing things right the first time.

You need to focus on your business, especially when you're taking orders. If there's any lack of attention, it could cause a financial crisis for yourself, your company, and your client. *So strive to produce error-free work; do it right the first time.* I believe that it's not only a good habit, but also a necessary one.

How can somebody tell if this business is for them?

You have to be comfortable in selling your skills and abilities in the market place. Be comfortable in picking up a phone and saying "Hi, my name's Bob Conrardy, and I just talked to your friend, John Doe, and he said I should be talking to you because you trade bond futures and one of my areas of specialty here at Cargill is dealing with bond traders like yourself."

Any other reasons for your success other than the ones already mentioned?

I think you have to be driven to do this type of work. This is fun, but it's also hard work, and you need to work hard to be successful. You are probably going to encounter a lot of rejection, but you can't let it get you down. There's always something new to learn in this business. Yes, you definitely have to be driven.

What about perseverance? Persistence?

You must look at this business with a long-term view. Being persistent when trying to build your business is, of course, going to be a good approach to handling business. There are going to be ups and downs for anyone in the brokerage business, but getting up and saying, "Okay, I need to continue to move forward" is something a new broker needs to do. He needs to consistently look ahead and say, "Where's my business coming from now and where will it come from tomorrow?" Another thing to understand about the brokerage business is that you'll probably lose about twenty percent of your business through no fault of your own. Maybe the client decides that using the markets is not the right strategy any more or maybe his company's financial situation changes, or maybe the client moves to a financial institution which doesn't use the futures markets or maybe moves to a career that is not involved in this industry. So you always have to be looking for new prospects, new clients, new ways to get business.

Do you have any war stories of how persistence paid off for you in opening an account?

Oh, sure. There is one account that comes to mind. I must have been talking to this prospect for about two years. It was a large bank on the east coast. I got along with one trader very well and would touch base with him on a regular basis. At the time, however, his firm didn't use futures, but I kept in touch with him because he was a good guy and knew a lot about the markets. He was also good for networking because of his industry contacts. Eventually he moved to a firm that did use futures. In fact, they used futures very actively in allocating money among different asset classes. Fortunately, when he went to the new firm, I was one of the people picked to do business with and he still does.

You mentioned east coast and you're in Chicago. Was it just a phone relationship, or had you met this person? Do you go out and see prospects and clients?

I do both. A lot of times you can use seminars and conferences as a way to meet your present clients as well as new prospects from all over. Once you've introduced yourself to a new prospect at one of these events, you might call them later and say, "Hi, my name is Bob Conrardy, I met you at such and such a conference and you mentioned you were involved in. . . ."

Any advice to formerly successful brokers who are now struggling? What would you say to those guys?

First of all, I think they need to ask themselves why they were successful. What was it they were doing right? Was it them or was it the markets? If the markets set up an environment in which everyone wants to trade and volume is high, I think the majority of the brokers in the industry are going to do well, but it will be those brokers who understand what really drives the client and is able to provide value-added service to meet the client's needs who'll probably do well over the long haul. Again, brokers need to find out why they were successful. Was it something they themselves were bringing to the table? Or was it that they just happened to be at the table when the food was being served? In the eighties, there were very good trending markets and a lot of brokers did well. Who knows what the future brings? A broker looking to get back on track has to do a little soul-searching.

Do you have any advice for people just out of college trying to make it in our business?

I understand that, for a newcomer, building credibility is going to be hard. What they need to do is basic stuff: keep up with what's going on in the industry, participate in educational seminars, do a lot of reading about the markets. When I started in the business, I think it was very helpful to have some experience on the exchange floors, learning and understanding what was going on in the pits. It really pays dividends; now when I'm dealing with clients, I can explain to them how the order flow takes place and some of the nuances a person outside the trading floor probably doesn't know or doesn't understand. So whether it's spending time on the floor, spending time at seminars and classes, or just spending time on your own reading books and articles, that's probably the best way to build up your knowledge and credibility. The next step might be to sit down and write out what you know. Ask yourself, "What do I really know about this industry or product, and what do I probably need to know in order to feel comfortable in talking with clients?"

I only have a couple more questions, Bob. Is there anything you wish you would have known or been told when you started out in this business?

Yes, the use of leverage. I don't mean financial leverage, but rather leveraging on other people's talents and skills. I believe you can learn about something quicker by talking to someone with experience than by trying to learn it on your own. Don't be afraid to ask for help. Leveraging on others' knowledge can help move you up the learning curve very quickly; for example, if I'm trying to learn a new software package on my computer, I'm more comfortable and successful learning it by finding someone who has used the software before and having them show me how they use it. I find that spending time with them first and then playing and testing the software myself is probably the best way for me to learn. Sitting down and reading the whole software manual is just not time-efficient for me.

Bob, your firm resolve, your drive, where does it come from? Something in your background?

I think some of it comes from both my father and my mother. In fact, sometimes I look back and wonder how my family got by financially. I realized that it must have been because of my parents' drive trying to provide the best they could for my brothers and me. Being from a large family, my mother's full-time job was taking care of the boys, while my father was a salesman. He worked at Sears selling appliances. He did his best to help put all of us through college, and they both encouraged us to strive for our goals. In fact, I know my brothers strive to do the best at whatever they're doing. Of my brothers, two are doctors; two are dentists, one is an architect, one is an engineer, another is an accountant, and the youngest is a software specialist.

Wait a minute. How many does that add up to?

I have eight brothers. I'm number seven of nine boys.

Wow. Are you aware of the Irish magic . . . you're not the seventh son of a seventh son, are you?

No, John. Nor will my wife agree to have seven sons (big laugh).

Carol Dannenhauer

Lind-Waldock & Company
Chicago, Illinois

Carol, could you please tell us how you got into this business?

It was 1978, and I was very bored working as a CPA. I thought I'd be good at sales because I like people. Sure, everybody says they like people, but I really do. So I answered an ad in the paper about selling and shortly after that found myself working for Heinold selling commodities—as they were called back then.

How did you start? How did you open accounts?

Heinold bought lead lists, and I'd just get on the phone and introduce myself and say I was with Heinold Commodities and ask them if they had any interest in commodities, and then start talking to them. Heinold had a pretty good research department, and they were well-known across the country because of their hog operation. So our name was not new to people—at least they had heard of us. I joined Lind-Waldock in 1986, after working for my brother on the floor of the Chicago Merc for a few years.

What did you learn from your beginning experiences that would help new or not-so-new brokers reading this chapter?

Well, you have to have a certain self-confidence. *This business is trying, stumbling, picking yourself up, and coming back and trying again. You've got to be able to handle the rejection. It's critical to remember that the person on the other end of the phone isn't rejecting you, so don't take it personally!* They're rejecting the idea of trading or maybe they're just having a bad day, but you can't let their bad day give you a bad day.

How do you 'bounce back' after you've been rejected? Any advice for other brokers?

Remember, I haven't been rejected—just my idea—and just for today—and just that one prospect. The next person I call might be waiting to talk with me. I think it has a lot to do with attitude, mind-set, and expectations. I read somewhere, "If you think you can, you can. If you think you can't, you're right." Most of all, you've got to be focused. Yes, getting and staying focused keeps you from dwelling on rejection, from feeling sorry for yourself. Being focused gets you going and keeps you going.

Any advice as to how a broker can get and stay focused?

I just know what works for me. I do some self-hypnosis and that helps. It's focusing on one particular thing you want to accomplish. It can be small or monumental. You can think, "Okay, this year I want to accomplish this goal." Or you can think, "Tomorrow I want to find out for sure if this particular prospect is going to open with me, *and if not, why not,* and what I could have done or do differently to get him to open."

The night before, I concentrate on what I want to do. I'll be by myself and try and get into a very quiet, self-hypnotic state and concentrate on tomorrow's situation. I try to see it in my mind going my way. Then the next day, I'll call that prospect and say something to the effect of, "You know, I really want your business, but I want you to be comfortable about it. I know you haven't made the decision to open your account. What is it that you still need to make that decision? If I can provide you with the information you need, then will you be able to make the decision?" Then you have to shut out all distractions, all other thoughts, and listen. Be there with that prospect and for that prospect.

What percentage of your time do you spend on the phone?

Only sixty to seventy percent now because I'm so involved with the needs of my existing customers. When I started out, I was on the phone eighty to ninety percent of the time.

How many calls should a broker make a day?

At least a hundred a day for a new broker. Most brokers, including experienced ones, seem to go in fits and starts in terms of prospecting and often don't prospect at all when things are going well—but often that's when you're best at it because you may be on a roll and have the confidence to do it well. Also, I try never to be away from my office between eleven and one because so many people call on their lunch hour, and I want to be available to them. Another time I try and be near my phone is between three-thirty and four-thirty because a lot of people are involved in the stock market and when it closes, they may be thinking about their investments and maybe me.

Any telemarketing secrets you'd like to share with other brokers?

I don't have any secrets. I just try to keep on going. Basically, what I try to do is get a feel for what time frame the prospect has regarding commodities. Have they done any homework? Have they already traded? If so, I ask them how they trade. Then I find out what they do. I try never to let anybody off the phone before I find out what they do for a living.

Why is finding out what someone does for a living so important?

Because nine times out of ten, it tells you exactly how much money or income they have. Now, sometimes you have to probe a little without the prospect feeling that you're being nosey. For instance, if someone says they're a builder or contractor, you might say, "Gee, if you opened an account and we needed to reach you, can you get to a phone if you're out on a job?" I want to find out if this guy's swinging a hammer on a roof someplace or what. Now your prospect might say, "No, my employees do that, I'm usually here in the office, you could reach me right here." You may want to go on to ask him what kind of houses he usually builds. If they're in the five hundred thousand dollars and up category, then you know you may be talking to someone with substantial wealth.

How do you ask the question?

I say, "What do you do for living?" That's a great lead in—then there are a million things you can say to them. One guy called the other day, and I found out he was in the flooring business. "Oh, gees," I said, "I'm remodeling this house, and I'm thinking about whether I should put in tile or hardwood floors." He said to me, "Well, you don't sound like you're twenty," and I said, "No, I'm forty-seven," and he said, "Then maybe not tile because it's really hard on your back, and the trend now is for hardwood, and they have a little more give to them, etc." There's nothing people like more than talking about their business. I then say how glad I am to have talked to him, and we develop a pretty good rapport. Yes, he opened an account.

You need to honestly, genuinely connect with people. I don't mean long life histories or anything, but I watch the weather report every morning when I get up so I can make appropriate comments about it. That afternoon I talked to this guy in Portland, and started in about the rain and how they'd been getting hit with it, and he started saying how he had all these problems with the rain and said he was just in a horrible mood. We had a little conversation about that and then went into talking about trading, and I said, "One thing for sure, if you open an account and start trading, then something else will occupy your mind and you won't even know it's raining."

This may all seem like insignificant small talk, but you have to give them just a couple of minutes of person-to-person contact to remember you by because many of your prospects will probably also be talking to several other brokers before they choose one.

How do you get people to open up to you on the phone? How do you get them to do the talking?

Well, I guess you have to be careful about the statements you make, but usually it's a question. Nonthreatening stuff. Some question or some comment to loosen things up a little. I figure I might as well enjoy myself as much as I can when I'm working because it's the biggest part of my day. You can't be silly, though— dealing with people's money is serious business. As I said, I ask people what they do for a living. *The most important part about getting people to talk is for you to listen—if you have to tape your mouth shut, do it! If you are going to be in this business, you have to shut up. You hear new brokers on the phone and many of them are running their mouths nonstop. You see what happens to these brokers—they very quickly leave the business. This I know for sure: prospects don't open with brokers who talk too much.* Sometimes, if you catch yourself talking too much, quickly ask a question. If the prospect remains silent, don't immediately jump in—wait a few seconds because chances are, if you don't say anything, they're going to go on. *It's hardest to keep your mouth shut with a prospect or client who talks slowly because you want to help them. You are sure you know what they want to say or are trying to say. Don't do it. Don't "help" them.* People like this are always having people interrupt them or finish their sentences because they speak so slowly. Let them finish their own thoughts. They will appreciate you for it. In fact, you may be the only one who does. *Bite on a pencil if you have to. I do, or I'll take a sip of water, anything, just to keep my mouth shut.* The only way you're going to find out what it will take to open someone's account is to listen, and you have to concentrate hard when you're listening. You can't be doing anything else, you can't be writing or playing with the computer or doodling. You have to listen. Listen to his tone as well as to his questions. A lot of times I can tell from the way someone is talking whether they're really a good prospect or not, but even to find that out, you must listen.

Also, you must speak in an honest, sincere, *not phoney* manner that makes people want to answer. You *must* put enough inflection in your voice that your prospects or clients feel that you *care* about their answers.

How can you tell if someone is a legitimate prospect or a waste of your time?

If a prospect tends to wander on about a "small talk" question that you've asked, that's not a good sign. Let's take the flooring guy, for example. If he had gone on to tell me about houses he had built, and other unwarranted details, then I would have felt, okay, this guy doesn't need a broker, he needs a psychiatrist.

How do you know how much money to ask for?

First of all, you should have already found out what your prospect does for a living. Also, if you can approximate his age then you can estimate from experience his net worth. This gives you a starting point. Ask him what he is interested in trading and ask for at least double the margin on each contract so he will not generally be bothered by margin calls if his positions go against him. I always suggest they post Treasury Bills as margin and this often gets them to open a larger account. Of course, you must keep advising your prospects that money put into futures must be risk capital. I also tell them that I feel the most important thing is to trade and manage their money with discipline, discipline, discipline.

Any other advice about opening larger accounts?

Large, small, any size, you must first identify your prospects' needs. Everybody thinks they're special. So I say, "What are your particular needs? What kind of charts do you need? Do you need floor access? How about evening trading?" Once you know what your prospects need *specifically*, it's a lot easier to open them. In fact, you can't sell anyone anything unless and until you know their needs. It's just basic selling.

Are there any books or tapes you would recommend to help brokers build their business?

I've read dozens of books on selling. I know you must be aggressive, you must do things a little differently, you have to stand out. I liked the tape by Og Mandino, *The Greatest Salesman in the World.* I also like the Wayne Dyer tapes—they help me maintain a positive mental attitude and outlook. I also do my best to stay away from negative people. People like to be around and do business with happy people, so I try to be happy (big laugh).

How about referrals?

Oh, I ask for them all the time. I tell my clients that a lot of my business is built on referrals and that I try to take care of all of my clients and service them well. People love to feel they're helping somebody. That's very important. If I'm trying to meet a specific goal and I have prospects on the edge, I'll call them and say, "If you're really thinking about opening an account, you could really help me out." Then I ask them to send in the check now, if they're going to be opening soon anyway. I've even had people call me back and say, "Carol, I'm really sorry, but I couldn't get my funds cleared in time."

How do you keep up with what's going on in the industry?

I go to conventions and I learn a lot from my clients, and of course, outside reading—maybe two hours a week. No, make that five.

Do you ever not feel like being on the phone?

Yes, it happens once in a while. So on that day, I come in and make sure I work—maybe I'll write letters to prospects or clients, maybe I'll read or do something productive so I can still feel good about myself when I go home that day.

How do you "ask for the check"? What words do you use?

I say, "When are you going to send me the check or wire the money and how much are you wiring?"

Just like that?

Just like that because, by that time, if I can't ask that person that question, then I have not done the work I needed to do to get there. If the prospect says, "Well, I really don't know," I say, "Oh, I'm sorry, I must not have done my job well. I thought we were ready to do business. Please tell me what else you need from me before we can get started." Your goal right at that point must be to find out why he's not going to open, to find out if there's a specific reason that you can't control, and to get him off the phone if you cannot meet his needs. *If your prospect is iffy, then you really want to spend some time trying to find out what he needs to open because opening those iffy prospects is what makes the difference between an average broker and a successful broker.*

Any other tips on asking for the order?

If the prospect cannot open at this time because of circumstances beyond your control, ask him when he might be in a position to reconsider. Agree on a follow-up time even if it is several months, and do the follow-up. Sometimes these are the easiest orders to eventually get. Be sincere about wanting their business whenever they are in a position to open an account and when they do open an account, the chances are good they will open with you if you have demonstrated to them that you are sincere about wanting their business.

A few minutes ago, you emphasized the word *discipline*. Could you please elaborate?

Discipline applies to brokers as well as traders. First, a broker must have the discipline of a daily routine, including making a

certain number of calls every day, and a monthly routine of set-
ting goals, reviewing goals, measuring goals. Then a broker needs
the discipline I talked about before of being focused on the job.
Forget the socializing and the office politics—that's probably the
hardest thing for most people.

I use the word "discipline" a lot with my prospects and
clients. They'll say to me, "Do you think I can make money
doing this? I know a lot of people lose money doing this. Carol,
what do you think are the qualifications to make money in this
business?" Of course, I tell them over and over that any money
they put in should be risk capital, and without exception I say to
them, "You know there are maybe five hundred systems out there
that could make money over time, but very few people who use a
system make money because they lack the discipline to follow the
system. Now, I'm not saying follow a system and the system will
make you money, but if you're a disciplined person and can follow a system of money management that appears to be profitable,
in my opinion you'll probably increase your chances substantially."

John, I think with people who are already successful in
their business, when you tell them being disciplined can probably
help them in their trading, they say to themselves, "Heck, I'm
already disciplined. I can do that!"

Carol, how do you handle the stress of this business?

Well, I guess I handle it okay because I don't perceive this business as being particularly stressful.

Anything else you'd like to add?

It all comes down to believing that your customer is the most
important part of the equation. You have to, and you can't be
giving lip service to that. The customer comes first. I think it all
boils down to that.

Bill Gary

Prudential Securities Incorporated
Oklahoma City, Oklahoma

Could you please tell us a little about yourself, Bill?

I was born and raised in Indiana. I attended Southern Illinois University, majoring in finance and math. While attending college, I worked for Union Starch and Refining Company, corn millers who made corn syrup and cornstarch. At Union Starch I was a cost analyst and eventually became a corn buyer. After working at Union for five years, I joined Longstreet Abbott & Co., a commodity research firm, where I could concentrate on futures research. I started at Longstreet as a trainee and ended up as their feed grain analyst. We did very detailed fundamental analysis, requiring a thorough understanding of the industry. That was about thirty years ago and I still do research in a similar fashion to the way it was done at Longstreet.

How did you get started in the brokerage business?

At Longstreet, we were not allowed to go into brokerage offices
or even associate with brokers. On my lunch break, I would go to
a brokerage office nearby and look through their front window to
check prices. I thought I knew more about grain markets than
most brokers, and they were making up to fifty thousand dollars a
year. A commodities firm, Barnes Brokerage Company, cleared
their trades through Longstreet and I eventually bought into the
company and joined their Dallas office. After moving to Dallas, I
decided to hold seminars to attract clients. I ran an ad in the
Dallas paper for a seminar, but nobody showed up. I later found
out that in Texas, they were called lectures and not seminars. My
next ad was for a seminar/lecture. About twenty people attended
and I opened three accounts that night—that's never happened
since. As you can tell, my start in the business was rough. I had
no idea what it took to open accounts, to anguish with people
when they were losing money, and—just as importantly, maybe
more so—to keep them down when they're winning.

At Barnes, I discovered that there weren't any good research publications, except those published by Longstreet. I had
the research experience gained at Longstreet and lots of research
material, so I decided to provide brokers at Barnes with a publication named Commodity Information Systems (CIS) that would
answer specific research questions. CIS was initially given away
to our clients in Dallas and Oklahoma City. Then we began to
receive calls from people who didn't want to switch their accounts
to Barnes, but just wanted to subscribe to the market letter. That's
how we got into the market letter business. We incorporated in
1969 and have been around ever since.

In 1985, I left the brokerage business to devote full time
to research, publish the market letter, and trade my own account.
I bought an advisory firm with more subscribers than we had at
that time. That gave us a circulation from coast to coast as well
as internationally. I spent all my time doing research and writing

the market letter, and our business grew substantially until the 1987 crash. In 1987, our sales were about $1.2 million in sub-scriptions alone. That's how big the business became.

After the 1987 crash, the individual trader began to disap-pear. I don't exactly understand why that happened, but I assume the crash scared people. Although brokerage firms sold com-modity funds before the crash, they really pushed them after the crash. Funds attracted many of the individual traders because they didn't want to experience that kind of risk again. After the markets went haywire in 1987, our individual subscriber base started to trail off. I had six full-time employees and kept think-ing, "It will come back, it will come back." The last two years, I took no paycheck—had no income. Finally, I had to admit we were going to be forced to cut back everything—rethink every-thing. So, in 1992 I moved to Oklahoma City and went back into the brokerage business.

How did you rebuild your business?

I rebuilt the business just as I built it twenty years before, with campaign trades. Although I had been out of the retail business for five years, I believed my experience and love for the markets would come across to prospective clients. Personally, it was tough for me to become a regular broker again because people don't often understand someone being in the business as long as I have: "A fifty-year old commodity broker is a rarity these days." Fortu-nately, the company didn't put me in the bull pen with the train-ees. So once again, I rebuilt my brokerage business and it has come back to the point that gross commissions exceeded $1 mil-lion last year.

Do you use your market letter as a prospecting tool?

Yes, that's how I build my business. We send a free copy out to prospective clients and they eventually give us a chance.

We also mail out flyers to prospects that contain a header like, "Don't know beans?" The flyer has a place for the prospect to reply for additional information on the soybean market. When they do reply with their phone number, we know they want to be called. We then have a chance at selling the market letter or opening an account. The reputation of CIS has also grown and we now open accounts by word of mouth.

Did you do anything else to build your business?

We normally develop a campaign trade. It's a long-term trade with good fundamentals and technicals, something we can live with and believe in for three to six months. We prepare a report on the trade with examples of how it can be traded, showing potential profits if the trade is successful and the expected loss if the trade is unsuccessful. We send the report to past, present, and prospective clients. We also buy name lists and offer it in a mass mailing.

Where do you get the names for your mailings?

We buy names. In the last three years, we have had a very good response with a list from a chart company in Florida. We've also always had good results with Commodity Traders' Consumer Reports, a California firm.

What happens after you develop a mailing for your campaign trade?

We initially send out a flyer, what we call a teaser, making sure we follow all the rules of balancing prospective risk and reward. In the flyer, we include a coupon and offer the prospects a free report. The report will be a full economic analysis of the trade with price and fundamental charts that allow them to see how we arrived at our conclusions. We also illustrate how they can approach the market from a long-term point of view, utilizing futures or options. Again, we are careful to point out risk as well as profit potential. Out of each hundred flyers sent out, we normally get back ten to fifteen responses.

When they request a copy of our campaign trade report, we include one more coupon that is designed for a second response—a coupon offering additional information. When they respond for a second time, we know we have a highly qualified lead. As with any broker, my most valuable asset is phone time. By qualifying my leads, I am able to utilize limited prospecting time the most efficient and effective way.

I don't try to open big accounts. I have found that opening five thousand dollar accounts is a very effective way to build business. We don't anticipate making a lot of money on a small, new account. We just want to cover our initial costs. We normally have about three chances to make a new client money. If we haven't made money after the third trade, we're probably going to lose the account. On the other hand, if we do make money on one or two of the first three trades, we then have an account that is worth more than five thousand dollars. Once we have a happy client, we ask for referrals and our business branches out and builds from there.

When you get on the phone with a prospect, how do you carry the sales process forward?

I'm not an expert salesman by any means. I believe sincerity is the thing that helps me the most. I love the business and trade markets myself; therefore, my enthusiasm and honesty about the perils of trading come across. The other thing is knowledge. Most prospective clients have little knowledge about specific markets or how they should approach commodity trading. If you demonstrate extensive knowledge about the trade you are trying to sell and have two or three alternative ways to trade it, the prospect realizes you know what you are talking about—you become more than just a salesman. The way to open and maintain an account year after year is by knowing your product, educating your client, and helping him or her stay within reasonable bounds.

What are 'reasonable bounds' for a ten thousand dollar account?

Normally, for a ten thousand dollar account, I don't like to see a position greater than three contracts. Our one objective with new five or ten thousand dollar accounts is to help them get a feel for the business—so that eventually they won't need to talk to me, but will begin to call my trading assistant with orders and requests for information. I go over every account's positions and equity each day. When people are over-trading or not managing their risk in a reasonable manner, I call and discuss it with them.

Any other advice? Any other trading rules?

Everybody's got an idea. There are a lot of books and pamphlets about trading commodities with rules you should follow. The bottom line is, you've got to have the discipline to manage risk. Risk management is my prime concern with a new account until they've been with us for a while and stop-loss orders come automatically to them. When they trade without a stop, the tendency is to wait just a little bit longer. It's just human nature. We try very hard to encourage stop-loss orders with all our clients. We have some large clients who don't use stops, but they have the money to back up their positions and I know that. I don't try to tell them what to do. The only reason they trade with me is for information.

How many contracts do you allow a five thousand dollar account to have?

I prefer one, until we get the education and stop-loss discipline in place. The purpose of a small account is to learn the market place. I'm investing in them—they're investing in me. Some of the accounts I have now were trading with me before I got out of the business in 1985. One has been trading with me for seventeen years. That's kind of old for a commodity account, but we know and understand each other. He started out as a five thousand dollar account. I've had a lot of five thousand dollar accounts turn into fifty thousand dollar accounts, and I've lost a lot of five thousand dollar accounts.

How much of an account's equity will you risk on any given trade? Do you have a rule of thumb for that?

No, I really don't. I tell people to be reasonable, and being reasonable to me is going up to fifty percent in margin, if something is really outstanding. Having been in the markets all these years I can sometimes recognize outstanding opportunities. Nobody knows what the low or high is going to be, and nobody knows the exact timing; but, when you see an outstanding situation, it's okay to risk a little more than normal on the trade. Usually one or two outstanding opportunities come around each year.

When we call our clients and give them the background on an outstanding trade, there's a tendency for them to want to really jump in with as many contracts as possible. They shouldn't do that. If it's going to be that good a trade, it's going to make the money we need to add positions as the trade unfolds. A good trade is going to last six months or so.

Do you pyramid?

Yes, I think that's a key element. Our initial position with a larger account might be four contracts. Then, if the market performs as expected, we add three, then maybe two more, then one. This is how we pyramid. We do have clients who will double their position at times, when everything comes together. You've got to have guideposts with these kinds of trades. A guidepost can be technical, but I'd rather it be fundamental. As the trade unfolds, there are times to press the position, knowing we're jeopardizing profits accrued in the base position; however, we don't fall in love with a trade, even though we've gotten to know it quite well. Also, we must be prepared to take a loss in the whole trade at this point.

Here's my best pyramiding story. I was regional vice president of the commodity division of E.F. Hutton back in the late seventies. An office manager in Louisiana called and said, "Bill, I've got a good friend who goes to Vegas once a month. He's never traded commodities. I'd really appreciate it if you'd take a five thousand dollar account for him and manage it. He's always wanted to trade commodities—I tried talking him out of it—but he's determined. So I said, 'If he's going to trade with somebody, he should trade with you.' " The client came in my office and said, "Bill, here's five thousand—if you lose it, there's no problem—it's one trip I won't make to Vegas. If you make money, I'm going to leave it in there, and you just run it the way you see fit." This was 1978, and we had been looking for a big bull move in cattle for months. I had bought cattle and got stopped out, and bought again and got stopped out, maybe three or four times. I had just about given up on the trade; however, the best trades always seem to come after you've just about given up. This new account came in at exactly the right time. He opened for five thousand dollars and I put three spreads on for him. When we got out four months later, he had over a hundred contracts and I gave him a check for one hundred and seventeen thousand dollars.

The odd thing about this client was, when his account reached fifty thousand dollars, he started calling every day. When it got up to about one hundred thousand, he started coming to the office. At the peak point, his account was worth one hundred eighty thousand. When the trade was over he came to the office, picked up a check for his balance, and never traded with me again.

He was so upset that his account went from one hundred eighty thousand at the peak to one hundred seventeen thousand by the time we had liquidated all the positions, that he never traded again.

When you trade for a big move and pyramid it, you're never going to get in on the low and out on the high. When we catch a big move, we wait for the market to top out and take back some of the profits—that's how we know the move is over. The worst thing you can do is to try to pick the top after you've gone through the gruelling experience of being there in the first place— then see the market go on without you. It's very difficult for the broker because most clients want to take profits. If a client gets out too early, the odds are high that he will want to get back in and that's when trouble begins—if the market turns right after he gets back in, it is extremely difficult for him to abandon the position and take a loss. I've seen traders give back all their hard earned profits because they re-established positions at a high price level and refused to take a loss when the market turned.

Bill, let's get back to your prospecting again. When you get these people on the phone, the ones who have sent back the two coupons, what do you say to them?

"Hi, this is Bill Gary with Prudential Securities in Oklahoma City. You requested a copy of our report on soybeans and I'm calling to see if I can answer any questions you might have." If they haven't studied the report, I tell them I'll call back in a week or so to help clarify anything they may not understand. I want them to have gone through the material so we can talk about it in detail. I want them to have the best possible understanding of why something should happen in the market and how they can utilize that information to their advantage. It's not unusual for me to talk with a prospect for up to an hour. I want to invest enough time for the potential client to gain confidence in both the trade and myself.

What do you cover during that time?

Most of the time is spent just answering basic questions: What's the best market approach for his size account? What should his overall goal be in trading commodities? Where does commodity trading fit into his investment plan? What should he be looking for in weeks ahead that will confirm the trade is on course? I want him to be left with the impression that we work very hard for our clients, because our success ultimately depends on his success.

We usually talk a little bit about their personal lives. I know people like to talk about themselves, so I just give them a chance. I ask them about their families and always let them know that my daughter, Denise, works for me. I've discovered that if you get personal with people they'll open up and feel as if they've acquired a new friend. I want to gain their respect and confidence.

What do you say to them about risk?

I approach risk from the most negative point of view—first! I tell them about eighty-five percent of the people who trade commodity markets lose money. Then I say, "But there's a good thing about that statistic. That is—fifteen percent of the people are taking away money from eighty-five percent of the people. That's why commodity trading, when its successful, can be extremely successful."

The primary reason that eighty-five percent of the people lose in commodities is because they have a limited amount of money they are willing to risk and once that's gone, they become a statistic. The people who make money, the fifteen percent, are still in the market.

The statistical heart of this thing is a little skewed. There are a lot of small individual traders who open an account for two or three thousand dollars and take their chance. If they lose, they quit and become a statistic on the negative side. The clients I want are those who are willing to work hard to understand the market. If they will work with us to learn, we'll work with them to understand the business. We'll have some bad times, but we're going to have some good times, too.

We've talked mostly about bad times. If we were to hit one of the good trades that come along every year or so, we could do very well. When that happens, I always advise a client to "draw down your money. Draw down half of what you make and put it somewhere. Don't put it with another commodity broker." We always try to get that money out of his commodity account to keep his numbers down until we get another good trade working. That way, if we have several bad trades in a row and we've gone six months without making money, the client has backup capital to use in the next good trade.

Would you rather be working with a beginner or an experienced trader?

That's a fifty-fifty. Experienced traders are like trading assistants. I don't like trading assistants who have worked for another commodity broker because I want to train them my way. Experienced traders have already developed their own trading approach and it's often not an approach I believe in. Some traders are "in-and-outers," people who trade very short term. I have never known any short-term traders who made money. I don't believe in this approach and I don't want these traders for clients for several reasons. First, I know I'm eventually going to lose them as clients. Second, if they stay as clients, they call ten times a day. Third, with this approach, they are going to lose money and that's not good for my reputation.

Is the nature of your business primarily spec?

Yes, I'd say eighty-five percent of it is spec.

Is it all over the country, or primarily in the Oklahoma City area?

We probably only have two accounts in Oklahoma. Our accounts are all over the states.

These accounts are ones you've opened by phone?

Yes, I've never met most of my clients. Probably ninety percent of our clients I've never met in person. Some have been with us a long time, ten years or more, excluding my five years out of the business.

Bill, I have a series of questions here entitled *Advice to Young Brokers About...* The first question is, what advice do you have for young brokers about prospecting?

Approach it from the idea that you're helping people. You're not a dealer in Vegas. You're here to build a business and to do a good job for them. Don't worry about commissions. I know we all have to eat, but keep your living costs down. If you're coming into this business, you probably have a guarantee for six months or more. Don't try to force the brokerage. Your purpose is to build equity, to build trust with your clients, and to become as knowledgeable as you can about the markets. Subscribe to different market letters, they're not too expensive. It's worth it if you get one good trading idea out of a market letter. You've got to believe in a trade to sell it. You can't sell a trade to people that you don't believe in yourself. Also, read and study your company's research if they provide it.

What if you're a broker who hasn't had a good trade in months? You've consistently been on the wrong side of the market? You don't feel very confident when you get on the phone telling somebody why they should do this or that.

That happens several times a year. I'll go through a bad spell and lose my confidence. Seems like everything I recommend is just a bit too early or a bit too late, and my timing is off. My clients get irritable, and I get irritable. So what I do is sit back and think of a long-term trade, like a campaign trade. I can buy December corn in late winter and feel very confident going through the summer period. So that's something I can sell and feel confident in. I don't have to be right next week. When I'm selling the same trade, selling a long-term perspective, I'm not going to do a lot of business near-term, but I can regain my confidence, and that's the key.

How about servicing an account?

I want them to have charts, if they want them. If they want a copy of a government report and we don't have it, we get it for them. We try to go the extra step. It's as simple as that. Go the extra step. If I've got a client who's in a bad position and won't get out, what can I do to neutralize this thing and stop him from a huge loss? I'm going to lose the account if I can't convince him to get out. I tell him, "There's always a trade tomorrow, but we're fighting this market." I'll take time to come up with some ideas that I can hopefully sell him on. While there are no guarantees, I'll look at options that may reduce his risk exposure. Then I'll run charts of the spreads, maybe I can help protect him some way with spreads. Again, no guarantee. It's horrible when you can't convince someone to get out and they're making margin calls every day. That's why we like to train them early with small positions, using stops that are placed when the trade is entered.

Mental stops get moved and can hurt you. Put in real stops at the time you put on the trade, especially with clients who you think may not want to get out if it turns into a loss.

There's a good research service we use a lot. They put out books of historical charts and seasonal trends. For our better accounts, I buy one and send it to them. There are several accounts I've bought a fax machine for. They are impressed that I send a fax machine, but I can get information to them fast that way. Everything we do is for markets. In other words, the reason I sent a client a fax machine is so I can fax charts or other things that will help him make decisions in the market place. Look at seasonal trades. If I were just starting out and had someone interested in soybeans, I would find a seasonal program that goes through fifteen years and picks the optimum buy-days and the optimum sell-days for the year; however, that kind of trade only lasts a few weeks. They're not long-term trades because there are too many things over a fifteen-year period that change. Let's say it's late November and the seasonal shows the best date for putting on the trade. It also shows the date you should cover, which in this example is, say, early February. So you have about a two-month trade. The trade gives you the history of maximum drawdowns, peak equity, and the ratio of probability. These things sell. It's an easy sell. They show the risk-reward ratio, historically. So you and your client have an idea of what the probability of winning is. If you're going to follow this kind of trade program, you've got to give the market room to work. So I'd rather see a client trade one contract than five—this gives us greater leeway for the stop. I've got a lot better chance of that trade being successful, particularly on a campaign trade. My objective is not to do brokerage and earn that fee. *My objective is to train my clients, conserve equity, to survive long enough to be around, and to still have money to trade when that once or twice a year real opportunity comes along.*

What trading mistakes do you see rookie brokers and rookie traders make?

I think the biggest hazard is hoping the market is going to come back. *Not using a stop, I think, is the single biggest hazard, and I repeat, it's up to you to sell your client on using a stop.* You can't make them do it, but if you want to build your business, then you've got to think along these lines. You don't want the first trade to be bad for a new account, but the chances of his closing the account are pretty low if you've been conservative and used a stop. If you've done a good job selling, he's probably going to stay with you for three bad trades. At least that's been my history. The higher the probability to make this thing successful, the better off you are. So it's better to trade one contract than five. Give the market a little leeway, but always have a stop. I don't care if it's twenty cents away and it's out of range. It's there, and it's going to be there next month. Once you've opened the account and the client's taken a position, he can call and get quotes from a trading assistant. Service your clients as needed, but you can't spend a lot of time with every client. You've got to go on to the next one. You've got to repeat the same process and sell the next prospect or client the same trade, and the next and the next. Keep going. Don't get lazy. *Sometimes after you've opened several accounts, there's a tendency to sit back and admire your work. Fight the temptation. Get going. You're on a roll!*

One more thing. By the time some prospects open an account with a campaign trade, it's two months later. Maybe the market's five cents lower. He just gets a better deal, that's all. So you improve your likelihood of having another client be a winner, if it's the same trade. That's the key. I sell the same trade. It's exactly the same trade every time. The more I sell it, the better I get at talking with people about it. The feedback and the questions they ask me tell me what they don't know. It's the sincerity, the knowledge of the market, the working with the client. I have as much interest in his making money as I have in making money in my own account. In fact, I probably have more. I take bigger chances in my own account because I don't have to explain to anyone.

You mentioned getting feedback from your clients. How do you get a client or prospect to open up to you? To talk to you?

You ask them questions. I ask if they received our latest letter. "Did you look at page so and so?" "Did you notice that chart?" I like to use pictures. People will look at pictures. If you can use charts to illustrate supply and demand, it will be easier for the client to understand.

How often do you call prospects?

I call them once in a two-week period, that's ten working days, unless you work on the weekends.

Do you work on weekends?

I usually work weekends; it's the best time to call people, particularly farmers.

So you work on Saturdays?

Yes, I usually work all day Saturday. If I'm calling leads, that's prime time. After seven in the evening is also good. During the day, if you're just starting out, work on learning about markets, getting your sales pitch together, writing your flyer, getting telephone numbers for the people you're going to call. The day is for organization. Evenings and Saturdays are for selling.

Ex-clients. Do you ever go after former clients who used to trade with you?

Yes.

Does that work?

Yes.

What do you say to them?

If they're ex-clients, they lost money on the last trade. When I call them back, the first thing I do is face the music. I tell them I know they lost money the last time, but I've got something I think they should be interested in. *They're the easiest people to resell.*

How so?

Because they want to make their money back. There's no better prospect than an account who has lost money and quit trading. You can tell him why we lost money before and how we can work to avoid making the same mistake again. There are always other selling points you can come up with.

Any more advice to young brokers about prospecting, servicing an account? How about honesty?

Tell the truth no matter how bad it is. Just tell the truth. If you can't admit your mistakes, you don't belong in this business. Because you're going to make a lot of mistakes.

If you start telling half-truths, you can get into a pattern. I've seen this happen. Brokers get in a pattern of shaving things. The market is going against the client and the broker tells him it's a cent higher than it really is. It's still within the day's range. It did trade at that price earlier in the day, but it's still not the truth. Tell him exactly what it is. If he's going to get mad at you, he's going to get just as mad tomorrow. There is only one way, and that is total, absolute honesty. There's just no other way to go in your sales pitch, too.

What about honesty in the sales pitch?

Honesty is one of the things I think impresses prospects most. They say, "How many accounts made money last year and how many lost money?" Usually I don't know exactly, but if it was a bad year, I say, "Last year was a bad year and I'll tell you why." I'm always honest. Sometimes it puts me on the spot, but I tell the truth and then come back with a positive statement that offsets the negative tone of the conversation. The reason people are still with me is because we've had good years as well as bad years. We're honest in telling them that we'll probably only have two or three really good trades a year.

Bill, how do you handle the stress in this business? Do you have any advice to people about stress and how to handle it? Or how not to handle it?

It's miserable sometimes. When you go through a bad period, you don't feel like doing anything. I don't like to talk to anybody unless I have to. But, I usually get out of it by facing the music. The first time you face a bad period, people yell, scream at you— they're mad; but they're right to be. They have to take it out on somebody, but, your ego is flattened. Right after the disaster, in a day or so, you must face the music. You call a bad deal a bad deal. Some accounts are probably going to close. Half of them may be questionable and a fourth may have always been with me and they're going to be with me forever.

I come back a couple days later and I call them again. I know I'm taking a chance they'll really chew me out. I apologize for having gotten caught in a bad market. It's funny how they respond to you. They come back and say, "Don't take it so hard," or, "Yeah, I was ticked off, but hey, I know there's risk." They try to comfort me. It's an odd thing, but it works in many cases. Every once in a while it doesn't work; but you've got to take the chance. This is a business of chances. *All we're risking is our egos—our clients are risking their money.* You can't be destroyed when you do things like this. As I said, it makes me feel better when all my clients haven't totally lost confidence in me. I know we'll come up with something, and we'll be a lot more careful about the next one because I want it to be right. Unfortunately, it's still a fifty-fifty chance—it could be wrong, too.

Do you have written goals or goals in your head concerning accounts, equity, personal goals, career goals? Anything in the area of goals you have to say to the brokers reading this book?

I think it would be very nice to have written goals, and I've tried this before, but they don't seem to work out. There is always something that changes them, circumstances change. Then I forget them, especially if things are going okay, *but I always have goals when I'm on the bottom.* Every time I get run over and have to rebuild business, I have goals. I know how many people I'm going to call and I keep count. The "no" answers don't count. I stay at it all day, unless it's after ten o'clock, until I reach my daily goal. I force myself to do it. It makes me feel better. My goal is to open a certain number of accounts in the next sixty days, and I'm going to make ten calls a day and go through this program. The accounts come. I'm very disciplined about this. Before sixty days are up, I'm normally back in good shape. Things are working, I call my old customers and they also rebound. Things are going fine again, then I forget about goals. I do have a general goal. When I was at Hutton and Shearson and now with Pru, I always want to be at least one of the top ten percent of the brokers in the firm.

Any advice about retaining an account even though it's losing money?

It is a lot easier to keep an account you've got than to open a new one. That's critical. You want to protect the business you have the best you possibly can. If I have accounts that are in losing positions and I can't talk them into getting out, I just tell them how I feel about their positions, and they relate to it.

They are my bread and butter, so I want to save these people. Once they're out of the market, they see more clearly, but as long as they've got a position, they are going to defend that position. There's an inbred bias. It's human nature. What I want to do is to get them to think. Get them to realize what they're doing.

Traits of successful brokers you've seen in the business?

You've got to love markets to really be successful. You've got to look at it not as a brokerage business, but as a fun thing to do every day. Every day's new. Something's going to change. Some days are bad. Some days are good. People who are really dedicated to markets are the most successful. They immerse themselves in the markets and the information and help their clients understand the things they understand.

You've also got to be a salesman. You've got to care about your clients. You've got to be honest. You've got to take care of the book work.

I've seen a lot of brokers who always come in late. They get there five minutes before the opening. They don't know what's going on and *a customer calls and says, "Get me out." So he looks at his equity run and sees he's long five cattle. So he sells five cattle. He was really long fifteen, but ten were in the wrong account.* Now he's got an error. Is he going to pay for it himself?

He's got bad decisions to make when he should have had no decision to make. Your client expects you to know what his position is. He expects you to know what his equity is. You've got to do your own homework. It doesn't take that much. I guarantee it will save money somewhere along the line. *If you've got a lot of accounts, make sure you have somebody competent checking things. Hire an assistant with your own money if you have to.* It's going to save client relationships. It's going to save you aggravation somewhere down the road.

Do you have any idea what percentage of your qualified prospects become your clients?

I think we open less than twenty percent of them. It ought to be better than that, really.

Any advice about telephone technique?

It's imperative that you be a good listener. This is important: your prospects are going to give you clues about what they want, what they need. All you have to do is fill their needs.

If somebody said to you, "Mister Gary, teach me how to listen." What would you say?

People always like to talk about themselves. They're very willing to talk about themselves, but you have to make them feel comfortable, ask questions, and be sincere. It's very obvious. I've seen people ask about their children, and they couldn't care less. "Hurry up and tell me so I can get to the next part." You've got to be sincere and really interested in their children. *I make sure I tell everyone that my daughter, Denise, works here with me.* If you get personal with people, they'll open up to you and they'll feel like you're their friend. You do want to become their friend, but it has to be genuine.

Any other tips on how to be a good listener?

Talk a little slowly. You've got to relate to those people, so I had to learn to talk a little bit slower. I've found in talking to a client in New York or California, they may talk fast, that's fine, but talking slowly works for me. It's helped. I'm not sure why. *I don't want the prospect to think I'm hurrying them up.* They sense those things.

What are some of the common objections and how do you overcome them?

A lot of people say, "Gee whiz, I knew so and so down the road and he lost his farm trading commodities." Then you say, "Well, that had to be a while ago because today it's difficult to get caught in those kinds of situations ... at least, you shouldn't get caught." "Eighty-five percent of the people who trade commodities lose money. Why should I trade commodities?" "Well, not everybody loses. Eighty-five, ninety percent sometimes. The important thing is to be in the ten percent category. It's simple to say, but hard to do." *When you get an objection, you just use what you know. It's not a rebuttal. If it is, you're going to become an adversary to your prospect. You can't do that. You've got to just make it flow and come back with very reasonable explanations for things.*

Any books or tapes that you can recommend?

Well, I like Jack Schwager. I wrote the cattle chapter for his new book. There's some technical stuff in it, but most of it is funda-mental. Jack did a marvelous job on this book. The first version is about ten years old, so he revised it. I also recommend

Schwager's other books, *Market Wizards* and *New Market Wizards*.

What else do you read?

I spend almost twenty thousand dollars a year on subscriptions. They're primarily used in our research office. We maintain a library upstairs where the newsletter is published. We subscribe to a lot of things. I like to thumb through things and get the essence of different articles.

Are there any industry trends that are affecting brokers or that are going to affect brokers?

Well, first is the global market place. For instance, cattle will probably become a global market before this is over. In fact, it already is one to some extent because we're exporting more beef. You've got to understand the global market place, number one. Second is managed money, the funds.

Bill, I'm pretty much finished. Are there any questions I didn't ask or any other areas you'd like to address? Two or three pieces of advice to summarize?

The first thing is to always go the extra step. If you're new in the business, people are going to ask questions that you don't have an answer for. I tell the people who work for us, and this is imperative, *don't ever try to answer a question the client asks if you don't know the answer. Tell him you'll get the answer for him, and that you'll get right back with him.* This impresses the client. The client's impressed that you're going to go to some trouble, get the answer, get back to him, and service him. The worst thing you can do is give him an answer that's wrong.

Anything else to put the odds in their favor of succeeding in this business?

Well, you have to get your name out to the largest number of people. You've got to stay exposed.

How does a broker get his name out?

If you have nothing but leads, get on the phone and get your name out. Then come up with a mail piece—and you don't have to promise anything, you don't even have to forecast anything—but come up with a unique one-page mailing piece that will attract people's attention. You can send out a thousand pieces of mail, but it takes a long time to make a thousand calls. Of the thousand pieces of mail, you may end up getting twenty good qualified leads. It's worth it. So do ten thousand pieces of mail. Do a thousand a month or whatever you can afford. That's what I'm always doing when business is down. Once your business is building, keep up the mailing.

Lastly, how do you "get the check"? How do you ask for the order? How do you get over that last hurdle that seems insurmountable for some brokers?

I just ask for it.

What words do you use?

Normally, I'll say "Do you want to get in this trade tomorrow? Or the next few days? If you do, we need to get your money and your papers in." It works.

You just ask for the order.

You've got to ask for it. Ask for the order, ask for the business. *They're not going to have an opportunity to make money unless they get in.* Plain and simple. I'm also not going to make money unless they get in. I'm also not going to make money if I over-trade the account. I don't think brokers intentionally churn, but I do think brokers like excitement—I've been there myself. You get in one market, then you get in another, and pretty soon, you're trading markets all over the place and that's a disaster waiting to happen.

One thing I think is important is to have a book that's a little bit diversified. Probably a third of my book is people who trade five times a year. Then probably ten to fifteen percent of our business is people who over-trade. They don't day trade— but they over-trade. When they over-trade, you've got to control them so they stay out of trouble. If you can *keep them out of trouble*, then you can keep them as an account and they're going to make you a lot of money. You can do about sixty percent of your gross on fifteen percent of your book. The other accounts are position traders. So we try to keep those three categories of accounts.

Bill, any final words?

The most important thing is getting through the bad times. Anybody can get through good times and there are plenty of good times in this business. It's a great business!

Ed Jernigan

Dean Witter Reynolds Inc.
Brentwood, Tennessee

Ed, how did you get into the futures business?

My father's a farmer, so I grew up on a farm. I went to school at Middle Tennessee State University. I started out pre-veterinarian, and about halfway through a friend of mine said, "I want you to take this commodity marketing course with me." He was in agri-business. So I took the course, and decided that even though I had a love for animals, commodities was a lot more fun than zoology and all the other courses involved in becoming a vet. So I switched to agri-business. The agri-business school offered courses in commodity marketing as it relates to farmers, and I did my senior thesis on soybean futures trading in Brazil and how Brazilian farmers hedge using soybean futures. When I got in the business, I decided to do cotton instead of soybeans because there

were probably sixty to seventy brokers around here specializing
in soybeans and only four or five brokers specializing in cotton.

How did you actually get into the business?

My fraternity, Alpha Gamma Rho, a social agriculture fraternity,
had a lot of alumni who were floor traders in Chicago at the Merc
and Board of Trade. They had a program called 'Career Day' for
people interested in the futures business. The fraternity alumni
who were on the Chicago Exchange floors or working with futures companies in Chicago invited one guy from each chapter to
come up. So I met a lot of people who were in the business and
got a couple job offers to go work on the Chicago Board of Trade
floor. Also, a little local firm here offered me a job as a broker. I
took that and got some of my father's farmer friends to hedge
their beans.

**Okay, your first job just out of college was as a broker. Talk
about that. Did you just get on the phone or what did you
do?**

Well, I hadn't ever sold anything, so I'm not going to be a good
example for this book on anything to do with selling.
　　　Like anything else I do, once I decided to do it, I really
got into it, researched it all on my own, read all the books and so
forth. Now, since I decided right at the start I was going to do
cotton, I looked for the best broker in the cotton business. I
found that Thompson had one of the best ones. He was an older
gentleman, so I said to myself, "I'm going to work hard so I can
eventually get a job with Thomson-McKinnon and follow this guy's
every move." That was my plan. I first contacted the Department of Agriculture and got the list of all the cotton ginners in
Tennessee. They were concentrated in the western part of the

state. I had a fraternity brother who lived in western Tennessee, so I asked him if I could stay with him every weekend for a while. During the week, I phoned the cotton ginners and growers and lined up meetings for the weekends. I spent weekends in west Tennessee, meeting with these people, and eventually got some pretty good cotton-farmer and cotton-ginner accounts hedging cotton. I got my production up enough to get a Thomson-McKinnon interview and got a job with them. That is what I consider my first big step into this business. At Thomson, the gentleman who was a cotton specialist wrote a commentary on cotton every day. I kept his commentary in a journal and studied what and how he wrote. I worked there for several years and built up my business.

How did you build your business?

I did the same thing I did in west Tennessee, calling on cotton farmers and ginners. I just expanded it to other states. I also started calling on cotton merchants in person about then. I'd call on people and keep on calling on them and basically things just began to build.

When you went to see prospects, what did you say? How did you get them interested in doing business with you?

I said, "I'm Ed Jernigan. I specialize in cotton, and I want your business in cotton, and I'll do whatever it takes to get it." I didn't get it. Most of the time, nobody would talk to me at first, but once I got in to see someone, I kept calling and kept calling. Persistence, I guess, is the word. I never really solicited for speculative business or anything like that, so it wasn't a hit-or-miss type of thing. I concentrated on one thing: I just wanted their cotton business in hedging. So, over time, they succumbed.

Why? They had their business elsewhere with other firms. How was it that you got them to come over to you? What did you say to them?

I don't know of anything magical, really. I just tried to base it on service, knowledge, honesty. I also understood the farmer mentality and all that work because my father was a farmer. I grew up on a farm and most of my family are farmers. I was able to put myself in the shoes of my prospects.

So you knew how to talk to them a little bit?

I knew how to talk to them a little bit, and I just knew some of the objections. I don't know exactly how I did it. I never had a sales pitch, I never had any sales program. It was just that I wanted to build a relationship with them. I guess that's what it was, relationship.

Ed, how do you build a business relationship?

John, first you have to have confidence, and to have confidence you really have to know what you're talking about. You must understand your prospects' business. I have extensive industry knowledge, I have thorough product knowledge. I started learning about my product before I walked out the door at college. Then all I did was go to people and say, *"I want your business, and I'm prepared to earn it. I'll always be honest. I know what I'm talking about. I can't tell you if it's going to go up or down, but as far as the other information is concerned, I can give you the best available, and I'm never going to sell you on a deal."* The only reason I got some of the business was that when I went to these people over a period of time, they learned that I wasn't calling on them saying, "Buy this because it's going to go to the moon." Eventually, they learned that I was calling on them not to earn a commission, but to earn their hedge business. It worked over a period of time. Sometimes it takes years.

What kept you going, in the beginning, even when you weren't making any money?

I guess I believed that I could do it. I had never failed at anything else, so there was no reason to believe I was going to fail at this. I just believed that over a period of time it'd pay off, and I guess it did.

Ed, what about appearances?

I would say that personal appearance and the general appearance of the offices are critically important. I came from a very poor rural area where we weren't really taught about all the proper business dress and all that kind of stuff. When I was in college, one thing stood out in my mind. I took a course my senior year in public relations. We had to read the John T. Malloy book, *Dress for Success*, and were given a test on it. Personal appearance in whatever you're doing is very important. That's your first impression. If a broker makes the effort to go all out and pay attention to that sort of thing and packages himself properly, then I think it makes a significant difference.

In the area of packaging, does the Jernigan Group have sales literature they send out? You have a newsletter right?

Right, but no, we don't have anything we send out. I'm a Dean Witter broker. I publish *Jernigan's Cotton Sheet*.

Please talk about your newsletter.

Well, my market letter started back in 1985 when I was at Thomson. I followed those guys and watched how they wrote market letters. I left Thomson to open an office for Maduff and Sons. They bought a seat on the New York Cotton Exchange, and I became their cotton specialist. They hired a public relations firm to come in and help organize things. I was writing a market letter and, with the help of the public relations firm, we named it *Jernigan's Cotton Sheet*. They did a public relations campaign on it in the trade magazines. That's how it got started. At that time it was a weekly publication. Now, we also put out a daily commentary called *Jernigan's Cotton Fax*. This is its tenth year. We don't send it by mail anymore. It only goes by fax, and it goes to all our customers around the world. We also sell it through American Agricultural Communications System Inc. (Farm Bureau Acres) and the DTN service, so we sell it to subscribers and send it to our customers.

Ed, over your shoulder I see a sign that says, "Teamwork: the fuel that allows common people to attain uncommon results." Can you talk about that a little, please?

Well, the only reason why there is something called the "Jernigan Group" is because of a group of professionals here that together handle our customers' needs. We have traders who sit at a trading desk here and talk to the clients. Each trader is assigned a customer and they're responsible for taking care of all that customer's needs, talking to them, giving them information, reporting breaking news, taking orders, reporting fills, and all that sort of thing. So the group tries to make sure we're handling every customer's needs. No matter whose customer is calling, they all help because everybody here gets paid on a salary plus a bonus sort of thing. Nobody's compensated directly for anything they're doing individually. They only get paid for their performance as a group. *We watch out for each other here.*

How about teamwork in an office where brokers don't have teams to work with? Is there room for teamwork in a typical brokerage office?

In the typical broker's office I would think there'd be some room for what I've heard called "broker associations." A lot of times, a broker won't be able to even afford his own sales assistant, so he's left at the mercy of the *Catch-22*. He stays in the office and doesn't go see customers. Or if he's out, he risks losing some of the customers he's got, but he has to go out to get new customers. Part of that problem is solved through broker associations in which two brokers can agree to help each other. So I would say there is a lot of potential for teamwork. That way, when you're out of town, the other broker can handle your customers and so forth, and you'll do the same for him.

Any advice to young brokers about prospecting?

My advice to young brokers would be, always remember to put your clients' interests ahead of your own. Build relationships. Find a group of people you can have some influence on according to your speciality. Do a good job for those people. That alone will help. They'll direct you to more prospects, more clients, more business, as long as you always keep their needs in mind. That's the way I look at prospecting.

How about servicing an account? What does that mean to you?

Our philosophy is, "The customer is number one." We always try to do what is best for him and always take care of anything he might want.

But how do you know how to service an account? How do you know what their needs are?

Even before we try to get an account, we do some research, learn all about that firm, what they handle, what their hedging needs are going to be. We find out all about them. We also ask them what they're looking for from us, what they need from us. We try to really understand their business, their needs. That way, if they come in and try to hedge in an improper manner, we at least tell them that we think, based on our knowledge, that maybe there's a different way this ought to be looked at, something like that. We don't talk down to them. We're careful not to insult them. Sure, you can show them how smart you are if they're trying to hedge incorrectly, but that's not building a relationship. You can help them do it right without being arrogant.

What about importance of a work ethic for succeeding in the futures business?

Well, when I first got into the business, the general tendency of many brokers was to come in at nine and to leave at one-forty-five after the market closed. Out of all those brokers I knew when I got in the business, I only know of one who's still in the business—out of about a hundred and fifty of them. *So I think, for young brokers—and I don't think this business is much different from any other business —you just have to make your job the number one thing in your life for a while. If that means working from seven in the morning till ten at night six days a week, if you approach it that way, it will work. If you don't, it's not going to work.* You look around at the world at all the big, successful people: a couple of them might have inherited it or gotten lucky, but the rest of them worked seven days a week, twelve, fifteen hour days to accomplish it. That's the way it has to be done.

Goals. How about goals or a business plan?

I think goals are very important. A person has to set goals. We set goals here every month and every year on new accounts we want to obtain. We sit down and look at every prospect in the business who is not doing business with us. We try to analyze why, and what we can do about it.

You do this labor intensive prospecting even though you're successful?

Well, we won't be successful if we don't do it because we'll go to sleep and get lazy and fat, and there will be another hungry little Ed Jernigan out there willing to do what the customer wants, and he'll get the business. Sadly enough, one of the things about our business is that it's based on what you've done for me today, not what you did for me in the past. It doesn't matter if you're the biggest broker in the world. *That customer still wants his needs to be met. If you don't meet them, a rookie will meet them, and he'll get the business.*

Any comments about listening?

Listening is the key. If you listen to a prospect enough times, he'll sell himself.

What does that mean?

By that I mean, instead of going in and telling him what a rocket-science genius you are as a broker, maybe you should realize that he is probably successful in his own field. So I try to approach the customer as if he's the rocket scientist because he's the one who is successful and has his own business. He is intelligent, so he knows I'm not a genius or I wouldn't be doing what I'm doing. I'd be a millionaire from trading and I'd be on an island some-where with my feet in the sand. *You have to listen to the cus-tomer.* If you build a relationship with him, which takes a lot of listening, he'll realize you're not trying to sell him on something all the time.

You said if you listen well enough, the person will sell him-self?

Well, a lot of times, prospects have in mind what they want to do anyway, and if you'll just listen to them, they will tell you their needs. Then show them how you can fill those needs and you'll get the business. *This is instead of your telling them what you think they ought to do all the time.*

I asked about the length of a work day. Within that, there's the topic of work habits. Can you think of any work habits that are particularly important?

Time management. There are only so many hours in the day, so you've got a choice. You can waste a lot of them and put in fifteen hours, or you can use your time wisely, and maybe accom-plish the same thing in seven or eight hours.

Do you have any advice about how to manage time? What pitfalls to avoid?

Your office isn't a social center. It isn't a center to read the paper, to catch up on the latest news. That can be done in the mornings at home, or at night. My idea is, when you come in, you start doing business; when you leave, you can start playing, but while you're here it's a place of business. If you develop that in your mind, then you feel guilty goofing off. You realize that every minute is dollars and cents. So if you want to waste your dollars reading *The Wall Street Journal*, so be it, but it'll hurt you over a period of time.

What do you do when a prospect says, "Gee, Ed, I already have a broker, don't bother me."

I think it's just persistence. You could say, "Thank you very much, I'll send you some information from time to time, maybe if you get unhappy, you'll consider us." This business takes persistence and time. For example, we called on this one large commercial unit, they told us that they never did business with anybody but this one large brokerage firm. I said, "Would you even consider us?" "No, I don't want to even consider it." Well, I steadily just sent them our material. They became unhappy with their other broker and called us. That made me particularly happy that we had kept trying. We prospected them for three years, from the moment we first saw them to the moment we opened an account.

Well, what do you do about the commercials who want to speculate, and a lot of them do?

Sometimes we don't know about it, and that's fine. It's their business. My job isn't to tell customers what to do.

What is your job?

My job, I think, is to keep them up to date with the most important information we're hearing worldwide; to provide that for them before anybody else does in the world, and make sure they know about it to make their own decisions. Also, I make sure we provide them with good execution.

How do you find out what's going on in the world?

I have a fax line and two business lines in my home. Carol, my number one trader, has a fax machine and two business lines in her home. Sharon, the number one bookkeeper, has a fax in her home. We work at night. When we leave here, we'll talk to our customers in the Far East to find out what's going on, what's being traded in the physical cotton market over there. When we come in here, we can tell our customers what we've heard has gone on overnight. So, we call our customers at night who are in different time zones and different countries and talk to them. If a customer has an urgent question, he calls us at home, sometimes even in the middle of the night.

You'll get calls at two and four in the morning?

Yeah. We have what we call the twenty-four hour number, and those are the two business lines that ring in my house and Carol's house. We give our customers instructions when they open an account. "These are personal numbers, they ring in our homes, so you're going to wake us up. So don't wake us up unless it's important, but if you have a need, feel free to call me at home anytime." They also call me on weekends sometimes.

How do you ever go on vacation?

Well, Carol and I rotate. I'll go on vacation and they'll be able to reach her, or when she's on vacation, they'll be able to reach me. So in general, it's just part of that relationship thing. If you're entrusting your money and your hedging with somebody all the way around on the other side of the world, you want to kind of know they're always available. At least somebody.

Any common characteristics of brokers who don't make it in this business?

I call it the hero division.

What's the hero division?

I just think there's a group of brokers out there who think that they can figure out the markets, instead of spending their time developing relationships and servicing customers. They spend their time trying to figure out the market. They think they're going to be smarter than the market. Well, if I were smarter than the market, I promise you, I wouldn't be giving this interview, I wouldn't be dealing with customers every day. I'd be on the beach with my dogs saying, "The heck with everybody." It's a major trait in those who fail because they think they're going to become market experts and beat the market.

Is there any way a young broker can tell if this business is really for him or her?

To be successful in commodities, people have to be quick on their feet. They need to be tough and not get their feelings hurt easily. *They have to realize that there are no shortcuts at all.* They have to be able to deal with a long, protracted, gradual climb to getting business. They probably should have had some other successes before they got here, and they've proven that those successes came about the right way—they happened over a period of time and they had to work hard. If they're not one of those people, if they're looking for a quick road to success, they don't need to be in commodities. I think that through the years, a lot of people who were big, robust, "romp 'em stomp 'em" salesmen got into commodities, didn't do the customer right, and ended up being failures. They're not the kind of people we need in this business.

Any closing comments?

I guess it would just be to say to new brokers that they need to plot a long-term plan. Don't ever deviate from that plan for short-term gains. Always remember to keep the customer's goal as number one. If you do that for a long enough period of time, you'll turn out to be one of the best.

The Donehie
Award

Jonathan G. Kra

January 30, 1987

Managed
Account
Reports

Jonathan G. Krass

Palo Alto, California

Please tell us a little about Jon Krass.

I grew up in Scarsdale, New York and attended Williams College, where I majored in Economics—which meant I was qualified to do absolutely nothing. After graduation in 1960, I knew that I wanted to do something in financial services and narrowed it down to banking, insurance, stock brokerage, and real estate. I eliminated banking because it would be a salaried job. I eliminated insurance because I didn't want to talk to people about dying for the rest of my life. It came down to real estate and stock brokerage. The investment industry provided much more training and opportunity than real estate, so I joined Bache and Company. In 1962, I decided New York was not for me, so I packed everything I owned in a '52 Ford and drove west. I went to work in San Francisco as a stock broker. After three months, I realized that a young kid who didn't know a soul couldn't come into San

Francisco and cut into that older, established community. Just to the south, Palo Alto was the heart of Silicon Valley, a much younger crowd. So I transferred to the Palo Alto office in May of 1962. I've been in Palo Alto ever since, and still love it.

What was it like starting out?

Smile and dial. Dialing for dollars. At first, I naively figured I was God's gift to the investment community and that people would call me up. Of course, they'd never heard of me. They didn't call me up. I did very poorly. They kept reducing my draw until it got to four hundred and thirty-four dollars a month, which was minimum wage at the time. Then, I went to work instead of just going through the motions. I started building my business by doing seminars and giving lectures.

How did you get people to come to your seminars?

I advertised in the *Palo Alto Times*. People came. I put many of them on at the local high school.

How many people came to your seminars?

An average of ten to fifteen.

Did you charge?

No. My hope was that in two hours, between seven-thirty and nine-thirty, I could impress them that I was honest, had a brain, and if they had to do their stock and bond business some place, maybe they should do it with me. That's how I built my business. I kept at it. *That's the secret to building your business with seminars . . . keep at it.* It takes work, and I find most brokers aren't willing to really work at it.

In 1967, a high school junior came to one of my seminars with his father. He eventually went on to Stanford and got me to start teaching a class there. I ended up teaching at Stanford from 1969 to 1985, sixteen years. After the first two or three years, I had about two hundred fifty students per quarter. I taught two quarters a year.

Now, take us through the process. After a seminar, what did you do to open accounts?

Well, over the course of the seminar, one night a week for three weeks, I'd mail them something once a week. Then after the seminar, I'd just say, "Is there anything I can do to assist you in your investment business?" I'd also ask for referrals. "Is there anyone else you know who might like to come to a seminar?"

By 1969, stocks had turned around and started going straight down because we were in a bear market. I couldn't buy a winner. My analysis showed that the economy was worsening and interest rates were going up. It was hard to find any stocks or bonds doing very well in that environment. Back then, U.S. citizens couldn't own gold and we weren't in the business of buying art.

So I analyzed my situation, my job, my career to date. How had I spent my time? I spent part of my time doing what I call "trying to be right in the market." By that, I mean doing research, reading, talking to my network of contacts. Then the other time I spent was what I called "business development." This is prospecting, making cold calls, writing letters, going out on presentations, writing articles, conducting seminars, asking for referrals. So I spent some time on business development and some time trying to be right about the markets. I figured if I spent all my time trying to be right, and none of my time on business development, I'd starve to death because I wouldn't get any business. If I spent all of my time on business development, and no time on trying to be right in the market place, I'd also starve to death because my clients' investments would go down. If I spent half of my time on each, I would not do as good a job as I could if I spent all of my time on one or the other. It was a *Catch 22*. I didn't want to starve and I didn't want to do a halfway job.

I asked myself, "Well, what do you want to do, Jon?" I really wanted to find people with financial problems and assist them in finding professional financial problem-solvers. That's the business I wanted to be in. So, after ten years of being in the business, I finally had defined what I wanted to do. *This is something brokers should do when they start in this business: define what they want to do.* I then surrounded myself with investment advisors and counselors who had various expertise and who were as smart or smarter than I was. Then I went about finding people who needed that expertise and introduced them to these experts. These investment counselors had to execute their business some place anyway. They might as well execute it with the guy who brought them the business. Some of the experts I surrounded myself with were people in my firm; therefore, I'd split the business with them. Sometimes the experts didn't do business with us at all, but on balance, things worked out pretty well. Life was good.

Well, when the stock market was going down and I looked to commodities, I sort of blended the two concepts. I had to find decision makers who would manage the futures accounts, whose self-interest was the same as the clients'—profits in the account— not the self-interest of commissions. This was in 1970. There was one Commodity Trading Advisor (CTA) registered in the state of California. I subsequently opened the first managed futures account at a brokerage firm with an outside CTA. Commissions were low, profits were high. Over the next couple of years, I introduced seven or eight accounts to this CTA. *In 1972, I took a six-week vacation. When I came back, I found out that while I'd been gone, I'd led the branch in production because of all the business these commodity accounts were doing! So, of course, I continued to develop my commodity business.*

Jon, when you're talking with a prospect as to why he should have managed futures as part of his investment portfolio, what do you say?

I talk about the ideas of John Lintner, the economist from Harvard. I talk diversification. I say, "What are you doing with your non-dollar investments?" "What percentage of your money is in commodities?" They'll say, "None." I'll say, "Hold on a second, I think the answer is one-hundred percent, because commodities is all there is. Your savings account, your stock account, and real estate investments are all dollar denominated; therefore, you have a non-diversified commodity account of U.S. dollars for your whole investment portfolio." So, I'd say, "We're not talking about putting some of your money in commodities. We're talking about putting some of your non-diversified dollar-based investment account into non-dollar-based commodities. *I want to diversify the commodity account you've already got, not put you into commodities." That gets their attention. Let me add, you have to point these things out not as a wise guy, but as someone who is sincere, straight forward, and honest.*

How do you convey honesty?

By saying "I don't know" easily. Nobody expects you to know everything, and when you're young, you think you know everything. You've heard the one about the guy who was amazed how smart his father got during the four years he was away in college. The more you admit you don't know, the more honest you seem. When you're asked a question and don't know the answer say, "Let me find out and I'll get back to you." And when you say you're going to do something, do it. If you have an agreement, keep your agreement. You communicate integrity by being honest. You communicate integrity by telling the truth. I am the Ethics Coordinator of the Managed Futures Association, the MFA. I'm proud of the fact that in thirty-three years, I've never had a client who sued me. I think ethics is the single most important thing in any business, especially the commodity business, because people assume the commodity business has a bunch of unethical people in it, and for good reason. There have been, over the years, unethical people in it who were featured in the media. Today, when I give a lecture to a local Lions Clubs about commodities, the first three questions include a question about Hillary Clinton. It doesn't matter what my subject matter is. It doesn't matter what I'm talking about. Within the first three questions there is a question on Hillary Clinton and cattle. People want to know about ethics in the commodity markets.

Jon, do you have any advice about prospecting?

In every community, there are program chairmen for Rotary, Kiwanis, Jaycees, Lions, lots of service clubs. They're in charge of finding someone to come in and speak for twenty minutes once a week or month, on something of interest with ten minutes of questions and answers. Now, if you're in our business, you should be able to find something of interest to talk about for twenty minutes. You ought to be able to talk about something to stimulate interest in commodities, in you, and in doing business with you.

Any other advice on how to find prospects?

Referrals are the very best prospects. I don't really believe you can go out and cold call for commodity business. Actually, many people you meet may be prospects, and managed futures are appropriate for many investors.

How can you tell if somebody's just stringing you along?

Ask him, "Are you stringing me along?" I say, "What barrier is there between now and your doing business with me tomorrow? For some reason you aren't opening an account. Why is that?

You either know or you don't know. If you know, you'll either tell me or you won't tell me. All you have to do is say, 'I know but I won't tell you.' That's okay, but if you generally don't know, let me try to help you find out. You don't trust me? You don't like me? You believe it's too good to be true? You believe it's not good enough? What mistake could you make if you said, 'yes' versus what mistake could you make if you said, 'no'? Are you concerned that I will run away with your money? Do you understand that it's going to be in a segregated account at a major brokerage firm? Are you concerned about confidentiality? What is the reason that we're not doing business? It's okay that we're not doing business. Just let me know if we're never going to do business."

How long do you prospect someone before you give up on them?

It depends upon how big they are and whether I like them or not. If I like them, I could prospect them forever because my income from the relationship is the enjoyment I get out of it. If they're very large, it might be worth it to prospect for a very long time, but the real bottom line answer probably is, until you know you're not going to do business with them.

How do you know if you are ever going to do business with someone?

You make it your business to know: trial and error, time. One way is to ask them. "Do I have the opportunity to earn your business?" Another question I ask is, "If I give you an idea and you're going to use it, will you do it with me or with somebody else?" In talking to prospects about investing, I have two jobs. One is to convince them to do something. The other is to convince them to do it with me.

What's your typical day?

My alarm goes off at five-eighteen. It doesn't go off at five-fifteen or five-thirty because there might be news or a commercial. At five-eighteen there's usually music, so I wake up to music. I'll be ready to roll around five-forty-five, six o'clock. Then, I'll either go down to the office or wait for the kids to get up and work at the house for a while. I'm on the phone, I'm doing whatever I'm doing, talking to people, seeing what's going on. I also do a lot of writing: memos, letters to prospects, clients, business development kinds of things.

Jon, how about sales training, sales techniques. Should brokers learn how to sell?

Absolutely. That's all they do for a living. They call it something else, but that's what they're doing.

How does a broker learn how to sell?

He takes a good sales course. That's what he does for starters. He reads Percy Whiting's book, *The Five Great Rules of Selling*. He reads twenty other books on selling. He learns to listen. He learns to ask the questions that get a prospect talking. He finds people who are good at sales and tries to emulate them. He sees somebody, a role model whom he'd like to be like, and says, "Could you do me a favor? Could you let me spend a day with you? I would like to buy you lunch, and I would like to spend a day with you because I think I can learn from you."

Any advice to the people reading this chapter on how to stay or get knowledgeable in our business? When we survey pros-

pects, a frequent complaint is that the typical broker doesn't know very much.

I'm in early in the morning, and depending upon my children's after school activities, I don't go home very often before six. So I spend a lot of time at the business, working, reading, studying. That's how you can become knowledgeable.

So yours is usually a twelve-hour day?

I don't work as many days as some brokers. I vacation a lot, but I'm usually here before most other people get in and I'm in here after they're gone. I work a long day. I love my work. One thing about my work is that it's not dull. It changes every day. The clients change, the economy changes, everything is changing all the time.

You've observed a lot of brokers over the years. Can you think of some traits of successful brokers?

I call it the three "I's": integrity, intelligence, and industriousness. They're honest, they're smart, and they work hard. Others have said it before me, but it's so true: the harder people work, the luckier they get.

How about traits of unsuccessful brokers?

They're time-wasters. They are not in control of themselves; they are victims. They don't take responsibility for themselves. They are not very truthful with themselves and others. They don't make an effort. This is not rocket science. This is not hard. It's not difficult. *If you're honest, reasonably bright, and apply yourself,*

you can make a success. It may or may not be a resounding
success, but if you work hard, you can make it.

Many futures brokers who were successful in the eighties are
struggling today. Any advice to that audience?

First of all, they've got to find out why. Look at their accounts
from the eighties. Who were they? Why are they dying today?
Now, I'm going to tell you some reasons why I think they're dying. One of the reasons is that the people who were doing business with them in the eighties aren't in the business any longer,
aren't in the market any longer. A second reason some brokers
may not be doing as well today as they were in the eighties is
because commission rates have come down. They may be doing
the same amount of business, but they're doing it for half of what
they were charging before. Third of all, to the extent that they're
counting on the speculator for their business, if the speculator
hasn't been able to do as well as published managed money has
done. The speculator (or his wife) says, "What am I in this for? If
I'm in it to make money and the managed funds are doing better
than I am, maybe I should get into managed funds." *In 1980 the*
managed futures industry was at a half a billion dollars. Today
it's more than twenty-five billion dollars. Well, that's about twenty-
five billion dollars that has either come from money that used to
be in futures or money that wasn't in futures at all.

That leads to the next question. Do you see any trends affect-
ing the future of futures brokers in addition to managed
money?

Retail commissions are still coming down. That's one trend. Another trend that I anticipate is the unbundling of costs and services: firms' charges will be more broken down and itemized rather

than an all-encompassing fee. But you still have to add value if you expect to be paid what you're worth.

What are some examples of "value-added"?

Maybe it's giving him a recommendation. Maybe it's sending him charts or joining him as a committee of two that makes the recommendations instead of allowing him to make them on his own. Maybe it's talking him out of a trade. Maybe it's checking his trading and saying to him, "You're trading too much," or, "You should have your stop closer," or, "You should have your stop farther away." Or, "You've got to have a plan," or "You have to use strict money management rules." Maybe it's saying, "You shouldn't be managing this money for yourself. A CTA should be managing it." My value-added is mostly on the managed side. "I can assist you in finding a CTA who's appropriate for you better than you could find one without assistance. Furthermore, I may be able to tell you when he's not doing very well and that you should fire him. You're going to do your business some place, and when you consider all the value-added that you get, my rates are relatively low."

Do you still prospect?

I have my mailing list. I always want to do more business. My marketing simply is having a high profile. It's going to conferences, it's being active in the industry and my community. It's writing articles. It's making speeches. It's serving on committees.

Why should people reading this chapter do all that?

Because they'll like it, because it's fun, because it will make them smarter and, eventually, richer.

Can it help them get business?

I think it does. I think everything you do helps you get business. There may be no *direct* relationship between good intentions and quality work on the one hand and job satisfaction and income on the other, but, if you put a lot of the former out into the universe, it seems to eventually come back many times over. At least, that has been my experience.

Michael   Pacult
Shira Del Pacult

Futures Investment Company
Fremont, Indiana

Michael, what's your background?

I grew up in Detroit and went to high school in Indiana at Howe Military School. I attended the University of California at Berkeley, majored in English and Zoology and had lots of jobs while working my way through college. Met Shira through a friend. After we graduated, we started a real estate development company, built single-family, detached, residential housing. Came into the credit crunch in the late seventies when the housing market collapsed, and I remembered reading in the *The Wall Street Journal* about people becoming millionaires in grain futures earlier in the decade. That stuck with me. So when we got into the illiquidity of real estate, I said to Shira, "Maybe we should be in something where we can be liquid in three minutes." I'd also been doing some trading in the meantime, some studying of the markets, so we decided to move to Chicago to get into the futures industry.

Shira, how about your background?

I grew up in Santa Rosa, California. Nothing special. Switched colleges after I met Michael, and attended Cal Berkeley. Like Michael said, in 1980, we moved to Chicago to get into the futures business.

How did you know anything about it? What was your background?

I graduated Phi Beta Kappa in Art History. When we were in real estate, I also put together art portfolios for investors. When we moved to Chicago, I went to the heads of the different commodity firms and interviewed them for their recommendations about going into this business. I met with about seven heads of firms.

They all would see you? What did you say to them when you called on them?

They were all very nice and agreed to have me come by. I just said we were starting in this business and what suggestions did they have. My key question was, "If you had my background, and with all you now know about the futures industry, what would you do if you were starting over?"

What did they say?

They all said pretty much the same thing. They said, "I would never write an order ticket. I'd find the best traders and let them do the trading for my customers." Then, I'd ask who were the best traders in their firm or the best traders they knew. So that's why I got into managed futures and also how we first got the names of some very good traders. Back then you only found out about good traders through word of mouth. They never marketed themselves or they were just trading their own accounts, so most people never heard about them. This was before the emergence of Commodity Trading Advisors, so that's what we did.

You were one of the pioneers in managed money?

Oh, clearly. The interesting thing was, after the interview with the first person, I'd say, "Well, who in the industry do you think I should talk to next?" That's how I got to meet other people.

Can you think of anything else they said?

Diversify among as many traders as you can. Keep your clients diversified.

How would what you learned in these interviews help the readers of this book?

I would say there's tremendous value in talking to people who've been in the industry, asking their advice. Find out about their background, how they do things.

What, call up your competitors?

No, in-house. If I were working for Merrill Lynch, I'd be on the phone to the head person at Merrill Lynch, asking for advice. I'd ask who else in the firm would be good to learn from. One of the keys to success for any broker is to associate with the best people possible. That comes through networking, talking to people, establishing relationships with people you trust and like. You come across a problem, an opportunity, a good trader, you can pick up the phone and say, "What do you know about this?"

What about an Introducing Broker in Tupelo, Mississippi? How does a two-person IB down there employ this technique?

If they're going to visit Chicago, I'd make appointments with the key people from their company, and the exchanges. They're a tremendous resource. The people at the top realize, "Small today, huge tomorrow." They may screen you out as a nuisance call, but if you present yourself in a credible way, the top people are going to be willing to talk with you.

Shira, what were your first weeks like in the business?

Well, Michael had been experimenting with a certain sales approach. Keep in mind, I had already interviewed those people, and so we knew we wanted to sell managed futures. I didn't want to be a broker in the typical sense. Anyway, I just applied Michael's approach. I was prospecting novices, and the response was excellent. You had to explain what futures were. It just took off from there. It wasn't slow. The leads were futures related. I never just cold-called someone: they had been sold a book about futures or they had requested information from the exchanges. More than anything else, I was never afraid to talk to someone I'd never talked to before.

How did you get over that fear, Shira, or did you never have it?

Unless it was my mother saying no, I just didn't take the rejection personally.

Talk about that a little. Many brokers we work with don't

like to get on the phone and prospect.

You never know why you get rejection. Maybe the person I called had just been told his wife was leaving him. Maybe it wasn't related to me at all.

Michael (joining in): There's a key though. When we are telemarketing, we have a rule: never permit anyone's negativity to enter our consciousness—we always keep a barrier up. If you're on guard when you're telemarketing and you're prepared ahead of time, you simply let any rejection bounce off. *Some brokers look at rejection as an excuse not to be on the phone.* Back to the point, we want information to flow from us to our prospects, not their negativity to flow from them to us. When someone is negative or rude—which isn't often—we never put down the phone. I keep the phone to my ear and immediately punch in the next phone call. Punching in the next phone call forces me not to dwell on what just happened.

Success is a combination of two things: first, conquer the phone. Second, you must persevere. The thing that's funny about this business is that you can call all day long and get no positive response, and then you say to yourself, "I'm going to make ten more calls, then I'm going to leave." You have three marvelous phone conversations, very high-quality responses. You're sending the people information, and you've had a great day. So you don't give up, ever.

Shira, any other advice to brokers about selling over the phone?

John, I don't know about anybody else, I only know what works for me. When I'm on the phone, I think very hard about what the prospect is saying to me. I'm concentrating two thousand percent. The second thing I concentrate on is making sure that what I'm saying is perfect, accurate. My goal is to have not one word off, one phrase off. I make sure I'm not speaking too fast, so they've got the freedom, the opening, the opportunity to bring up their comments, their questions. *No one wants to feel rushed or ignored.* And if there's a long silence, one of my favorite questions is, spoken gently, "I'm not a mind reader, what are you thinking?"

Michael, would you elaborate a bit on that philosophy, please?

The presentation must take the listener along an educational path in a systematic way without causing them to get out of step with you because you said something incorrectly earlier. You can't be on point C while they're still thinking about point A. Flaubert took twenty years to write *Madam Bovary.* He would spend days on one sentence to get everything perfect. We try to make our presentations perfect. We work on these together, to educate the prospect methodically and thoroughly, *always making plenty of room for them.* We go over the disclosure document, which is basically our presentation. We go through it in a systematic way that answers each prospect's questions in a prioritized fashion regardless of how the document is laid out. *You also must address their agenda, not yours.*

Shira: Total product knowledge is a must. Now, that doesn't mean you stay off the phone until you have total product knowledge. You're going to learn about your product through the questions your prospects ask. When you have total product knowledge, you're calm, you're listening to what the person is really saying. You'll be able to tell by their silence that they have a question. Then you just say, "Do you have a question?"

How do you get the people to open up?

By not talking too much.

Please talk about that.

Seriously, that's key. *If there's a secret in this business, that's it: listen.* Listen for intelligent questions. Expect them. You'll get them if you listen.

What do you say about risk?

I always go over the risks with people immediately. I go over the risk disclosure statement. I say, "You know, you could lose your principal. There's no perfect trading system, you can have a margin call. This has to be discretionary income, that if you lose it, you do not have to change your life style. This cannot be your bread and butter money." I cover all of those things with everybody.

Shira, how may hours a day are you on the phone?

I work sixty to seventy hours a week, and Michael's working the same so we're pretty much around the clock. Whatever amount of that is on the phone, maybe ninety percent, it's never enough.

Doesn't your ear get sore?

You just have to wear tiny little earrings.
M: Shira uses a headset.

Michael, what do you think is important? What does someone reading this chapter need to know to succeed on the phone in this business? Is there anything else you can think of?

You need to be a student of human nature. You need to like people, you need to be interested in people, you need to be constantly examining yourself. You have to know what makes you tick, what makes human beings tick . . . what their fears are, what their desires are. You have to understand human nature and you can't do that in the depth required to be successful unless you like people.

Shira?

I really like to come here and talk to people during the day. I told Michael if this wasn't my job it would probably be my hobby. In fact, if I'm home for too long, I go nuts. Even on vacation, I've got about five days I can stay at home before I want to get back to work.

When you talk of being on the phone do you talk to them about personal things, is it all business, or do you find out what they do or if they're married or have kids or any of that stuff?

You respect their time. You respect them. People can tell if you respect them. You never call someone on the phone and say, "Hi, how are you?" That's offensive. When someone calls me up and asks how I am, I say to myself, "What does this guy care for? Who is this idiot?" I'm ready to hang up the phone.

What do you say when you get people on the phone?

I say, "I'm Shira Pacult from Futures Investment Company," and that I'm calling about a futures program I want them to review.

If your prospect says, "Futures! Boy, that's too risky, that's not for me." What do you say?

I'll say, "Let's look at exactly what kind of risk it has; why don't you review this information and see if you're comfortable with that level of risk?"

Anything else about how you work over the phone?

It doesn't mean you are abrupt or curt with them, but you respect their time. *You don't talk to them like you're best friends.* You're not best friends. Now, some of our clients have developed into very good friends over the years. We have clients who are still with us from the very first year we were in business, but this is the process that comes along in time. When you're first talking with someone, you want to tell them why you're calling. You want to get right down to it. You want to send them something that could educate them, that you could call them back about and go over with them. In our case it's simply the disclosure document of the CTA we're recommending.

Michael, anything to add here?

Some prospects don't know how to say, "no." A professional telemarketer doesn't talk to someone who isn't qualified. So in your conversation, you need to determine if they're qualified to talk to, if they've got the capital, the temperament, and the interest to trade.

Mike, how do you determine if they're a good prospect on the first phone call?

We don't, because that puts a barrier up. *We do not qualify on the first phone call.* We assume if they are interested in receiving the information, there's some interest there. In the second phone call, we'll determine if they've got the financial capability and the temperament.

We don't just say during the first phone call that we'll send you something. What we say is, "we're going to send it to you and when you've received it, we will call you and go over it with you and we'll save you quite a bit of time just by highlighting it for you." We don't expect them to read anything, so the first phone call is, "Let me get my appointment book out and set up a time for me to call you back and go over the disclosure document. What works for you? Next Thursday? Fine." They tell me a time, I write it down, and I'll call them back at three o'clock on Thursday to go over the information. So, when we call back, we say, "This is Shira or Michael Pacult from Futures Investment Company. I sent you the information on Joe Jones, CTA, and this is the time for our appointment to go over the information together. Do you have it there in front of you? On the left side of the folder is information about us and our company, but let's go over to the right side, to the heart of the matter, to the trader's track record. Let's see the kind of return, the volatility, and the risk that's involved to make that kind of return. Now go to page twenty-eight in the disclosure document and let's look at the track record." Then we'll go over the details, they made this much this year or lost this much, etc. "Now let's turn to page fourteen and let's talk about the trader and his background." We go on to what makes him special. What's his background, what's his trading system, what does he trade, all of those details. Then we go to the fee structure. What's it going to cost you to do this? That's the next question. "So let's go to page twelve and go through the fee structure. There's an up front fee, a selling commission, and in a minute we'll get to what you get for that. Here's the management fee, the percentage of profits to compensate the trader, here's the amount you need to invest." We walk through the whole thing so they know exactly what they are looking at. We'll say, "Go to page one, circle that page and go back and read it at your leisure. It's a very important page, it's the risk disclosure page."

At some point we say, "A worst case scenario exists in absolutely everything you do and the worst case scenario exists in this investment also. You need to weigh the probability of its occurring." We also always say to people, "There's a fifty percent cut off. If a trader loses half your money, he doesn't deserve to lose the other half. We'll have him get you out as fast as prudently possible, but there are no guarantees." We've told them about locked limit markets. They can always call us up and find out what their positions are, and their account balance to the penny. We tell them they're going to get daily statements and a monthly summary.

What do you tell prospects about your service?

We tell them we monitor the traders on a daily basis. I've got almost twenty years' trading experience, so I know what it takes to be a successful trader.

Michael, what do you look for when screening a CTA?

First, I know how difficult a job it is. I don't have problems with losses. We've educated the clients so they shouldn't have problems either. I do have problems if the trader starts to deviate from what he initially told me he was going to do. So in the process of selecting a trader and deciding if we want to offer him to our clients, I ask them questions about what they trade, their trading philosophy, how much they're managing, how many accounts, what's their worst draw down, what's the range of loss, what's the range of profit, what's the average loss, average profit, how many times they trade per month. I ask a lot of questions, but the question I start out with is always the same, and it's a very simple one: "Tell me about your trading system." *If within ninety seconds I don't hear something about controlling the risk and capital preservation, I know I'm talking to a trader with whom I don't want to do business.* Because of the leverage and the volatility, you cannot succeed in this business unless your main focus is money management. I don't care if you've got the greatest system in the world: if you don't have any money to trade because you've blown the clients out before the system kicks in, your system's worthless.

Another thing, if all a trader has ever traded is the ags, and all of a sudden he's long a hundred silver, I'm all over him, even if he's in profits. If something doesn't seem right to me, I'll get on the phone with the trader to find out his thinking. We once had a trader we were using who had spectacular returns in a once-in-a-lifetime bull market in the bonds. I was happy and comfortable recommending him, but when I got the daily sell signal on the bond contract he was trading, I said to Shira, "Call and find out his thinking." He was not concerned about it. Then about four trading days later, I got a weekly sell signal, and I said, "Call him up," and Shira called him up and talked to him and we got the same story. I said to Shira afterwards, "Pull every client. That's it. Call all the clients in the next twenty-four hours and tell them we can no longer recommend this trader; we're nervous." Now, they could go on hold with him, or they could trade for liquidation, but I wasn't happy with what I saw. Sure enough, we got everybody out but one client who was a childhood friend of the trader. The biggest tragedies I've seen in commodity futures have always been through, "Oh, I know him personally." This client went from fifty thousand basis to sixty thousand, to under twenty-two thousand, and back to thirty-four thousand, but the rest of our clients didn't go along. So the monitoring and the time spent is essential. The other part of my job is very simple: help Shira to stay on the phone.

Michael, please talk about account size.

Well, twenty-five thousand and up accounts are harder to raise. You could probably raise a hundred fifteens in the time it takes to raise thirty twenty-fives. In the same amount of time, you would probably raise four or five fifties. So there's a point—this gets back to human nature—there's a point at which people, if they have the capital, will say, "Well, I'll try it," and then you're off in establishing a relationship in which you bring them other products. If it's fifty thousand you're prospecting for, a person looks at it and thinks, "It's real serious money." A five, ten, or fifteen is more like, "Well, I'll give it a try. Pacult and the trader seem to know what they're doing."

What are some of your products?

We are probably eighty-twenty individual managed accounts versus funds and pools right now. In the next two years, we will be the opposite. Eighty percent funds. We're forming our own CPO and we will be availing ourselves of this larger universe of CTAs with larger minimums by pooling people with smaller amounts.

Shira, you mentioned 'accredited investor' during lunch. Could you talk a little about that, please?

On the first call, if it's appropriate, I say, "Are you an accredited investor?" They'll say, "Well, what does that mean?" "That means your net worth is over a million dollars or your annual income is in excess of two hundred thousand dollars for each of the last two years." If they say they are, then I know I may have other programs that may be suitable for them.

Michael: Along the way, we've explained what we do. They know we don't just have one trader. They know we have a range of traders. If you're talking to someone who you know has a hundred and fifty thousand to invest, it's in his best interest to be with three or four traders rather than just one. You can lower the potential volatility if you are more diversified.

Shira, how do you "get the check"?

There is often some urgency when you're selling a closed-end fund because the fund may fill.

But what if it's not a fund?

Good traders fill up.

Michael: If there are four hundred brokers soliciting for one good trader, trying to get as much client money with him as they can, you have to communicate that to your prospect.

Shira: A lot of times you sit here and you think, "Gee, he's not going to fill up, but it does happen. I'll never forget, I was representing this trader and his cutoff was twenty million dollars, and he closed.

Michael: When we have a trader of this caliber, several things happen. One is, so much money comes in that he's no longer available. The second thing that can happen is that he raises his minimum so he's no longer available for twenty-five or fifty thousand. Great traders don't stay available when everyone wants to be with them. It is our job to educate the prospect to this possibility.

So how long do you keep prospecting someone, Michael?

The saying is, "Either they're going to die or we're going to die before we give up." In one month, Shira opened someone who was seven years in the talking stage, another person who was five years in talking. It's a matter of building rapport and trust, until the prospect is finally comfortable with us and the investment.

How often do you contact prospects?

Shira: When they tell me to. One person told me, "I'm just starting this business. Call me in three years." He thought I would
never call him. Of course I called him in three years and he's been
a good client for a long time.

Michael: If someone isn't ready to buy, you always say, "When
should I get back to you?" The person may say, "My CDs come
due in ten days, call me in a week," so never make assumptions
about when someone will want to talk again.

Shira, what's the average length of your phone conversation?

Three lengths. The first, three to five minutes. The second, fifteen to forty-five minutes. The closing call takes as long as the
person needs. On average, a couple of hours, not all at once.

Where do you get your leads?

One source of leads we have found to be helpful is business owners. Also, technically-oriented people. Doctors. Systems analysts. Computer people. People with analytical minds. Engi-
neers.

What's an intelligent way to work leads?

*If you spend Monday, Wednesday, and Friday calling leads, and
do your call backs Tuesday and Thursday, you're forcing yourself to spend sixty percent of your time prospecting. That's how
you should do it. You wear one hat one day, your prospecting
day, another hat the other day, your second-call, closing-call hat.
It makes more sense. It's easier. You don't have to keep switch-*

ing back and forth from one call to the next. Another thing with cold calling: if you're really on a roll, you should be able to do fifteen to twenty-five an hour. Very brief conversations.

How often do you communicate with your clients?

We always tell them to call in as much as they have the time or the interest. We also call them. It depends on the clients, their needs, wants, and size. We try to touch base with all our clients at least once every two to three weeks.

Let's address honesty a little bit, Michael. Any comments?

Honesty is the cornerstone of a person's character. It is the single most important thing. Life is challenging enough without making it more complicated by being dishonest. We don't deal with people who are dishonest. We don't have time for it. We just don't bother with them. In our business, dishonesty develops with this fear of being the bearer of bad news. It goes back to, "Did you educate your client properly from the very first moments you started talking to him about the risks inherent in futures trading, and that even the best traders might only be right twenty percent of the time?" If you've done your job right, you should never be afraid to call your client and tell him what the news is. There aren't degrees of honesty. You just are, and you don't make a big deal about it.

How about stress? How do handle the stress of this business?

Exercise is real important, whatever it is. Shira has an exercise machine in her office.

How about goals, written or otherwise?

Michael: Imperative. Short-term, long-term, intermediate, daily, hourly, decade-long goals. Write them down. Imagine them, envision them.

Any advice about selling, how to be a sales person?

Get on Nightingale Conant's mailing list. They're in Chicago. Shira's a big believer in listening to sales tapes, motivational tapes, success tapes.

Shira: Anyone in this business should read *Think and Grow Rich* by Napoleon Hill. If you want to succeed, you should know the qualities he writes about: burning desire, perseverance, the mastermind principle, etc.

Shira, if you were going to advise somebody on how to be a good salesperson, what would you say?

The first things are discipline and consistency. Next is working out a method.

What's your method?

Basically what Michael explained tonight. The three-step process, organizing your business. First phone call, sending out documents, second call, sending out applications, third call, the closing call.

I read in an article on selling that the most successful people working in McDonald's restaurants are ex-farmers be-

cause they are used to doing particular things at certain times, preparing the ground, planting seeds, fertilizing, harvesting, etc. That's what I would say: if you have some mental discipline, train yourself to do what needs to be done in a systematic way that works for you.

Anything else you'd like to add?

Michael: Because I work so much, one time *somebody said, "When are you going to get a life?" I said, "This is my life.* I'm not waiting to do something else."
This is on the cutting edge of knowledge, and if you're not plugged in to all these things, *The Journal,* watching CNBC, reading *Futures Magazine, The Economist,* news wires, business magazines, technical analysis, trading methodologies, you're in the wrong profession. You have to keep up with what's going on. The clients do. It's a never-ending learning process, and what's more wonderful in life than never to stop learning?

What about traits of brokers you've seen who don't make it?

Michael: We hired an equity raiser one time who was a very successful computer salesman. He failed miserably at this job because he couldn't sit and do it. He was used to setting up the appointment, getting out of the office, calling on people, socializing with them, that was his method of selling. To sit at a desk all day and dial drove him nuts. People fail because they don't like the job. This job is sitting, dialing, listening, learning.

There are futures brokers who do that, who call on people in person, but it's not what we do.

Shira, is there a difference in the way you prospect someone who has traded before as opposed to someone who hasn't traded before?

No. We still go through everything. Even though they know the risk, even though they cut us off and say, "I know this, I've traded before," we say, "Well, let me hear myself say it for my own sake, if not for yours, so I know I've said it. If you've forgotten anything, you'll be refreshed." You have to disclose everything, particularly the risk part—to novices, experienced traders, everyone—whether they want to hear it or not. It also helps build credibility.

What about people who have been in the business a year, a year-and-a-half, and they're struggling. How can they tell if they should stay in the business or get out?

I would say there's nothing in the futures world easier to sell than public commodity funds. It's there in black and white.

Why is selling public funds easy?

It's limited risk, you'll never have a margin call, they can get in for as little as five thousand or even two thousand. They've got the prospectus there: public funds are a wonderful way to get back into the saddle of soliciting, having a great product with a low minimum. Then you'll find you're not just opening twos and fives, but tens and fifteens. It'll start going up. I think finding a product you believe in is the best way to get back in.

Anything else you'd like to add?

Michael: The advice we got those first weeks in Chicago was priceless. Here were the presidents of futures firms who had seen it all, and without any prompting, they all gave Shira the same answer, prior to managed futures even existing: find brokers who can trade, never write an order ticket. Refer everyone to them.

Diversify your clients. Let them handle the trading, you stay on the phone. That's tremendous.

Anything we didn't cover, anything you'd like to add?

Michael: Don't waste your time, don't get involved with office politics. Come in to do business and be very single-minded about your activities.

Shira or Michael, any closing words?

Michael: *First of all I'd answer that by saying there's never been a time in the last fifteen years that has been better for futures than now because of the markets and the availability of professional traders. The second thing is, there is more money out there looking for a home than ever before. If you thought it was easy or hard before, you haven't seen anything yet. This is our heyday. This is the dawn of futures being understood as a valuable addition to a person's portfolio, of being accepted by people with the capital and the temperament. It's been like the stone age for us before, so if there were ever a time to succeed as a futures broker, this is it!*

Shira: *The final and maybe the best reason this is such a great business has to do with self-awareness, self-development. That's why it's so emotionally satisfying. You can't do this job and not learn about yourself. You're confronted every day with your weaknesses, your strengths, your fears. This job downright forces you to confront yourself, to be constantly growing and improving. People aren't going to remember you for anything material, but for what kind of person you are. That's what really matters.*

Marshall J. Persky

Merrill Lynch
Chicago, Illinois

Marshall, could you please give us a little of your background?

Sure. It's nothing special. I grew up in Georgia in a middle-class family. I had a couple of different jobs while growing up. Then college, work, back to graduate school, and instead of completing my thesis, I went to work for a big processor as a hedger, which was a wonderful experience for me. I liked being called a "hedger." Initially, I did not have much latitude, and in reality I was just an order person. The months the futures were traded were determined by a management committee. After a short period, timing was left to me, whether to buy or sell during the course of the day. I hedged soybeans, corn, wheat, and a little bit of oats. This was like achieving a Ph.D. because I received the experience and credentials of having been a futures trader for a major soybean processor.

Also, I learned about cash trading because I was sitting in the middle of a group of physical merchandisers. It gave me a perspective from the ground up, which has served me through my entire career.

You've been in our business a long time, and you've seen a lot of brokers come and go. Any observations or advice to new or even not-so-new brokers reading your chapter?

Listen, I'm going to tell you something about a lot of brokers in our industry—something that doesn't get talked about very often. Many brokers and would-be commodity trading advisors shower themselves with glory about what great traders they are. That's just so much nonsense. They think it's important to foster the belief they're infallible, they know everything, they have some magical touch, they're bigger than life and everything they touch turns to gold. People know all this posturing is just so much baloney and they can see through it. *You had better bring some humility to your job. The markets humble you anyway.*

If you don't sell yourself as a good trader, how do you sell?

I market myself in a different manner from most brokers. I maintain a client's complete anonymity. I don't exaggerate my accomplishments. *I tell people what I truly feel, and they know there is never any conflict of interest because I'm not spending time trading my own account.* I inform people very early in our relationship not to choose me as their broker to do their trading for them. If I were a successful trader, would I continue to take on the burdens of a broker? Clients select me as someone who can service and handle their accounts, who can execute well, and who knows where to find answers to questions they may have. I've been called 'The Ferret' because I relentlessly search for and dig out information for my clients, not inside information, but information relevant to their needs, even though it may be hard to obtain. Also, my clients don't have to worry about my not being accessible. I'm always available to them: long hours at the office, three in the morning at home, on vacation.

My business has been like a child, and while my child has matured and may not need as much nurturing as before, I still check its health on a regular basis and keep it healthy. That takes constant attention and work. When it comes to work, there are no substitutes, there are no shortcuts.

I've heard you say that in some cases, large clients should have more than one broker. Why?

It's true. One broker cannot have sufficient knowledge about all the various markets. I'm a dying breed—many of the brokers who now enter the business specialize. I still enjoy this business by following many markets, and because of that curiosity, I'm required to do more reading than I prefer. I like to keep up with the various markets because there is a relationship, an intertwining. This is a phenomenon young brokers may not recognize because they haven't had the experience, and I perfectly understand this. It's imperative to realize you can't give each client everything he needs. Clients also grow. Early in a client's relationship you can service his requirements. As he matures and wants to do other business and different types of markets, you aren't serving your client's best interests if you continue to do what's not in your area of expertise or talent. I'm talking mostly from the very large speculator point of view. Commercial institutional firms have multiple brokers and they have specialized departments.

What does it take to be a good broker?

I really don't know. Many brokers really don't understand the brokerage business. They don't think, they only conceptualize. There are so many different facets to what makes a good and successful broker—there aren't any one or two elixirs. You have to keep a mental index of many relevant items. A good broker has to be true to himself and must not delude himself that he is the most talented there is—because there is no best. He also has to be honest with his clients in many different respects. *If he recognizes that a client could be better served with another broker, he should tell him.* The broker would be surprised that his recommendation could bring him a lot of new business, but most brokers don't want to part with existing business. Of course, I'm speaking in terms of the success that I've had. Sure, there's been a lot of hard work, but also a fair amount of luck and serendipity.

Marshall, any advice about how a broker should continue to maintain contact with a prospect?

Advice? I'm not sure. I can only tell you about some of my experiences. Once I was in Myrtle Beach, South Carolina, attending a soybean convention. It was raining cats and dogs. I was under a canopy waiting for a cab, and another man came out and started to talk to me. We spoke for about twenty minutes waiting for our cabs. We exchanged cards. He was president of a large processing and consumer foods company. He introduced me to his senior hedger, but we didn't do any business for two years. I spoke with her once a day, then a couple times a day, then three or more times a day. I had the perseverance to call with information. I distinctly remember the first time I did a trade because I didn't do another hedge for nearly six months. Nothing wrong. They opened a small account with me, and tested me. After this period, I became one of their largest brokers.

A couple years after that I received a phone call from the same president. He had a client in Iran who wanted to do some futures business. As a result of standing out under that canopy, I met a major agricultural interest who was a client of mine for many years, and those Iranians have been clients of mine for over twenty years. Now we're close personal friends as well as business associates.

So how long should a broker prospect? Here I had hundreds of conversations over a couple of years before I wrote my first ticket. I was patient. *People don't like pushy people.* You have to use common sense about who's really a good prospect and who isn't.

You mentioned earlier you do a lot of reading. What do you read?

I read, review, and peruse dozens—and I mean dozens—of newspapers and business journals, reports, newsletters, research articles, not to mention numerous news wires. I also learn and derive much from my clients. It's not sufficient for a broker to simply read the business sections. It's important to know what's occurring in the world so you can try to interpret and relate certain events and hypothesize what market effect various situations may cause. If you don't know what's transpiring around the world, you'll be too narrow and shallow in your discussions with your clients, and they'll know it right away. *The kind of clients you want are globally aware, so you'd better be, too.* A lot of times clients or prospects will want to talk about subjects that relate peripherally to their businesses. For many years, agriculture— grain and soya—was a large part of my business and whereas I used to concentrate in that area, I have become very diversified over the past fifteen years. Many of my ag clients want to know about other markets. So I talk about interest rates, stocks, and currencies, etc., and how these markets may affect their businesses. And financial clients want to talk about grains. This is important: *if the clients want to know something, I will not give them half an answer or speculate just to get rid of the question and move on.* I tell them, pure and simple, "I don't know, but I'll try to get you the answer." This is how you begin to build a trusting relationship. *You say you'll do something and you do it.*

Do you trade your own account?

Not trading my own account is the biggest boon that happened for my business. Another reason I've done well is that I've recognized, as I mentioned earlier, that I'm not a superior trader. I don't have the killer instinct. My success in the brokerage field reduced the time dedicated to trading. The time devoted to servicing clients and fulfilling their requirements left little opportunity to consider a dual role as a trader. I look for other people to trade my clients' money and my own money. Those Commodity Trading Advisors (CTAs), some new, some young, and some who are older, have the drive and are trying to make successes of themselves. They perform well through different market scenarios. Selectivity and careful monitoring are paramount. Just as all trades are not winners, all CTAs aren't winners.

      I seek bright, energetic, aggressive people with various backgrounds: chemistry, physics, engineering, political science, economics, whatever. I have watched several become some of the greatest successes in our business. To succeed as a CTA, you don't have to have a financial background, but you must have control. You must be able to manage risk. *You have to know that there's a stop point which is more important than a go point.* If you don't stop enough times, you can never go again.

What do you look for in a CTA?

I need to know the makeup and parameters of his trading. I want to make sure his successes are not just options-related. I want to know the breadth of his experience. I want to know the type and frequency of his trading, as costs could become an issue during trying periods. What are his drawdowns, his ratios? I don't want my clients to spend money for CTAs to prove themselves. Let the money managers learn from someone else's money. When evaluating or starting with a CTA, I first think about how much money I can lose—not how much I'm going to make. I used to make that mistake, but now I control my losses because I know where my cutoff is. *That's what it's all about—controlling losses. Your first loss is your least loss.*

I want patient clients and money managers who don't want to be home-run hitters. That's a problem. Nearly everybody wants a home run. *Home runs are nice, but they are usually made by people with a lot of strike outs.* Today, in money managers, I look for singles and doubles. Over a period of time, fifteen to twenty percent compounded can become a tremendous amount of money. I don't look for the big hitters anymore. I don't want to have to work to try to make back the money.

I want to know what kind of person the money manager is, and I have a network, so I can find out, "How intense is he? Does he consume it, eat it?"

Do you think a new or even not-so-new broker should trade his or her own account?

No. Not at all. You've got to do one thing well. If a person is really a good trader, he should be a trader, not a broker. It's easier to be a good broker than a good trader, and it's not that easy to be a good broker. It's work.

If you had to start again. . .

I'd drive a yellow cab.

Have you ever refused an account?

Yes. Yes. Yes. Many times. For various reasons. They shouldn't be trading and I tell them, or I couldn't provide the service they wanted, just didn't like them, or the account just didn't feel right. You pay a heavy price for taking on a client you don't mesh with.

Any advice on the telephone part of our business?

Yes. First, the word is "yes," not "yeah"! Use "sir" or "ma'am." Etiquette on the phone is imperative. Chewing gum is an absolute no-no. People have to use common sense. They must speak with proper grammar and with intelligence. Getting a person's name right seems an arduous task to many brokers' assistants or secretaries. Learn to listen and pay attention. People want to be treated with respect. Get the spelling of the name and the pronunciation correct.

If you're having a problem executing an order, the client doesn't have to hear the argument—put the phone on mute. When someone calls, if you're busy, tell him so, but try not to sound harried. When your conversation is completed, return the interrupted call. One of my pet peeves is that some people don't call back at all, or in a timely manner. Perhaps their compensation is dependent on the number of meetings they attend. When people call you, they're entitled to a prompt response.

How about the importance of listening? Could you please speak about that?

I used to, and still occasionally, have the problem of not being a very good listener. I would tend to anticipate the question, like a guessing game, to show the person on the other end of the phone how smart or quick I was. I spoke before the client had completed his or her thought. Well, an objective in this business, any business, is to give others a chance to show how smart they are! Age and experience have made me a better listener and therefore a better communicator. No matter what they're talking about, I try to listen. A lot of times a broker becomes a father-confessor. You're listening to many non-business discussions. In cases like these, you may have to call back to listen, if you're busy with real business—but call back.

What have you learned from your successes—or failures?

From failures, *I've learned different answers to a variety of problems, and to think of losses first and gains second.* I have a lot of humility.

There's one thing I haven't previously addressed that brokers have to do. When brokers solicit a potential new account, they must understand the proper time horizon in developing the business. The process of developing new relationships varies significantly among different types of prospects. Many brokers think they deserve instant success, and if they don't acquire business in a short time, they stop soliciting the prospect. I have had several situations where *it's taken me one to two years to do my first order.* I don't pressure prospective clients.

I've learned it's one thing to be right—it's another thing to be able to trade right. It's not only forecasting the direction of the market, but it's also finding out that the train route usually has a lot of stops and detours, and you have to learn how to get on and off board. You have to have patience with the markets. Markets are like elections, and the markets always win.

What's also important to remember, when business comes your way, is that you may not know what you have. By that I mean, I have started off with some clients who traded only one contract or two or three. An initial three-contract trader became one of the most successful and largest commodity traders in America. Another small one- or two-contract trader has retired after becoming large and trading several hundred contracts at a time. And still a third small trader became one of my major clients within a couple of years. I have several ongoing accounts who are only trading two or three contracts. They are getting their feet wet—they have to learn. They may turn into a one-of-a-kind diamond, something unique. *You are introduced to some*

small accounts, treat them well, they progress, and they may be-
come giant accounts. Many accounts don't start large and they
don't give you any indication they could become huge. Some
accounts test you first, and many brokers fail the test; therefore,
the brokers don't receive the plum. I've been very fortunate.

Do you have any special work habits?

As I was building my business, I was all-consumed. Sixteen–
seventeen hour days were common. I was fortunate my wife,
Joyce, put up with my unfair work habits. No real vacations,
maybe a day or two or three on very rare occasions. I've been
successful, but paid a price and also made a lot of mistakes.

**Do any mistakes come to mind that other brokers reading
this chapter could learn from and maybe avoid?**

Several times in my career, I've had to make a decision about
clients. *If I couldn't adequately service a client, I was honest and*
recommended that client would be better served by a different
broker. I mean, it's not fair to my other clients for me to struggle
with a time-consuming, non-productive client if another broker
could handle the account better. I have given, without charge,
major names to other brokers to handle.

Many young brokers don't know in what direction to go:
hedge, institutional, retail, managed accounts. This business has
changed so much, you have many new experts and rocket scien-
tists. It is difficult to compete with some of this talent. I tell
prospects, "I'm not your man, but I've got the person for you."
That's how you achieve more business—yes—from the broker
you introduced this prospect to *and* from the prospect you turned
over. When they have something in your forte, who do you think
they trust now? Who do you think they are going to call? Who
are they going to tell other potential clients about? A major source
of business is references from other professionals. Trusting rela-

tionships, employment changes, and long-lasting associations are prime contributors to a growing business.

How about the stress of this business? How do you handle it?

You just walk through it. It's more of a conversation piece than reality. I just bite my lip, mutter to myself, and go through episodes. C'est la vie.

Anything else, Marshall?

It seems to me many brokers' greatest shortcoming is their failure to do the work themselves. They cannot solely rely on others to be their eyes and ears. They have to put in the effort themselves. You have to be willing to put the time and the study in, and if you have the patience and work at it—you don't have to be brilliant—success will come to you. You don't have to be a specialist in every area; although, today, it seems you have to be a specialist in some field.

The individual broker is going to be a thing of the past. It's going to be teams and groups. Instead of just being on their own, brokers will have to join with others because commodities have become a multifaceted, twenty-four-hour-a-day business. If brokers want to advance in the lineup, the way the game is now and is going to be played, they will have to have the willingness to join with others.

If someone decides to specialize, any suggestions?

If I were a young broker entering this business, I would look at the managed account area because I believe this field still has tremendous growth. If a person recognizes that he or she is not cut out to be a trader and realizes that there is a whole spectrum of people who are competent traders, why not merchandise their success and specialize in that area? *It's easier to sell another's*

proven trading ability than your own because if you were a good
trader, you wouldn't be a broker. Traders should trade and bro-
kers should broker.

This last question has to do with your personal philosophy...

A line of poetry has stayed with me for many years, and it's appli-
cable for this business. The quote is from Tennyson's *Ulysses*:
"To strive, to seek, to find, and not to yield." That's what I have
done. That's the philosophy I've brought to this business. I strove
to be successful, I have worked long and hard. I literally gave up
family, time, and a "normal" life. Sleep was and still is a luxury. I
was a workaholic and still behave that way. I have forgotten how
to relax. I used to enjoy playing cards in college. Three years ago
was the first time I'd played in over twenty years.

   I was fortunate I had the internal motor to be driven, but it
didn't start when I was twenty-one. What really got my engine
going was *my* decision to graduate from being a broker's assistant and market letter writer to becoming a broker on my own.
This self-reliance was also motivated by the constant remembrance
of a saying I was taught as a young boy. "If I am not for myself,
who is for me? If I care only for myself, what am I? If not now,
when?" It felt good to stand on my own feet. And as my business
grew, the material rewards were gratifying and allowed me to do
some good deeds.

   So whatever set of circumstances occurred, they happened,
and I have had some degree of success. Was it luck? Driven and
able mentors? Bright, skilled, industrious, and talented staff? Timing? Hard work? A good wife? Wonderful children? Undoubt-
edly a good measure of each!

John Roach

Roach Ag. Marketing, Ltd.
Perry, Iowa

John, would you please tell us a little something about your-self?

I grew up on a farm southeast of Des Moines near Carlisle. My family farmed grain and livestock. I was the middle child of five boys, and since my dad had a full-time job in addition to the farm, we all had plenty to do. After going to the University of Iowa, I went to work for Northwestern Bell. One of my accounts was a brokerage firm that did commodities as well as securities. I decided to get into securities, but a friend in the business told me commodities was where the action was, so I joined Lincoln Grain. That was in 1973. The timing was lucky because commodities were starting to take off in seventy-three, and the stock business was in real trouble in seventy-three and seventy-four. From there

I spent four years on the cash side of the business working primarily with farmers.

Then what happened in 1978?

I started my own company.

What's the nature of Roach Ag?

Our niche is transactional business, working principally with farmers and ranchers. We deal with about one thousand customers scattered across thirty-some states and several foreign countries. It's principally in corn, beans, wheat, cattle, and hogs. We handle business in all the different commodities, but we feel like those are our niche markets.

How did you build that business?

Well, I started it clear back in the seventies, doing seminars in 1973. I happened to be fortunate: my immediate supervisor, Laverne Halverson, taught me early on how to do seminars. After I was in the business for six months, I was out doing meetings. Of course, everybody was an "expert" in 1973. The people who were truly experts were the ones who were most often wrong, and for those of us who didn't know any better, it was easy to say beans were going to nine or ten dollars—we thought they could. So I think I was really fortunate to have started in that particular year because it gave me a real wide-open kind of a feel. *Seminar business was really the mainstay of how we developed our business in the beginning, and it's been that way ever since.*

What advice do you have for other brokers on how to do seminars?

The premise you have to start from is, as a broker, you wear several different hats. The number one hat, as I see it, is being a salesperson. If you structured your day in such a fashion that you spend (I'm going to be a little ludicrous) ten minutes analyzing the markets, and another eight hours doing the sales job, you probably would be a very successful broker. If you were to increase your market analysis time from ten minutes to two hours and reduce your sales time to six hours, you would probably be a less financially successful broker. So the whole process is one of taking a large group of people and separating out those people who want to do business with you.

Do prospects pay to come to your seminars?

Yes, any one we do in the office, we charge fifty dollars for them to attend.

And how long is the seminar?

Four hours, usually. Money-back guaranteed, and nobody's ever wanted their money back.

So how do you attract a big group of people?

There're a lot of different ways to accomplish that, and we've gone at it several different ways. We've done very small seminars where we've had people around our conference table. This is an excellent method: you start out with a group of people and you'll convert a substantial percentage of them into customers. Because they're sitting in your office around your conference table having an opportunity to interact with you for a period of two to four hours, they begin to feel they know you, and that's how trust develops.

For another approach, we go to other agri-business people, principally banks, and offer our services as seminar leader. Then we let the bank, elevator, insurance company, or farm management company find people for us and invite them; then we come in as analysts. We weren't endorsed by those people who sponsored us, but obviously they wouldn't sponsor a meeting and invite someone they didn't trust. So there is some implicit trust there.

What happens at one of these seminars?

First of all, you must understand the process. You're not there to sell anything. You're there simply to talk about something that interests the people attending and to give them some idea about your personality. It gives them an opportunity to form some opinion about whether you're the kind of person they would like to do business with if they choose to do business in the futures markets. The thing that's always hard for a broker to understand is that not everybody who comes to the meeting is a candidate to do business with you. You have to separate the non-prospects from those who are the prospects.

How do you identify prospects?

You have to call them. You call them and visit with them and ask, "Do you trade?" If they don't trade, then the next question is, "Do you have some interest in trading?" If they say "no" to that, then you have to create that interest or decide that there's not enough time to do this or try to sell them something else.

What else do you try to sell them?

We publish a weekly newsletter that assists in grain and livestock marketing, and we also will market cash grain for customers on a limited power of attorney. We know the people who attend these meetings have an interest in grain and livestock or they wouldn't be there. More specifically, in grain and livestock prices. So our first job, then, is to figure out who has an interest in grain and livestock futures, and secondly, is there something we can do for those other people who are not interested in becoming involved in futures.

How about telemarketing?

Let me share with you some of our numbers. We find that out of one hundred telephone prospect calls, we open five accounts. Now, we have to be a little bit careful on how we count these numbers because each broker has to make his or her own decision: "Do I call this person for the eighth time, the ninth time, the tenth time, the fifteenth time?" So it may well be that of one hundred phone prospects, there are five people you are calling twenty times each. Now, that's not quite right, either, because we usually don't call somebody twenty times. We tend to want to do business in the first ten phone calls. We'll try to shift from futures sales to a different product if it takes longer than that. We try to sell them our market letter so we can get our foot in the door with them and start to establish a rapport. Through buying our market letter, the customer indicates that he is somewhat interested in doing business with us.

How much does the market letter cost?

One hundred dollars a year. One page, two sided, published every Friday.

A lot of brokers struggle with trying to decide whether a prospect is legitimate or not. When you call those one hundred folks, how do you decide? What advice do you have to brokers about how to make this decision?

That's a very difficult decision; the first part of making that decision is, have they traded in the past? Are you going to work with people who are brand new to this business? If you're going to spend a lot of your time teaching novices how to trade, it's going to take a tremendous amount of your time, and you're going to have a difficult time making the kind of dollars you're going to want to make over time. That's not to say you shouldn't take on a novice, but you shouldn't give a novice fifteen to twenty phone calls unless they have a tremendously large business. There's a series of questions you need to ask, and in our particular niche, a major question is, "How many acres do you farm?" That's a little like asking somebody, "How many dollars do you have in a savings account?" Those are questions you have to be cautious about asking or you're going to offend the person. If you're working in a niche of wealthy individuals, what you want to find out is: "How many dollars of assets do you have that are investable assets?" but you can't ask him, "How many dollars do you have in a savings account?" So some way or another you have to find the answer to the question, "Do you have the wherewithal?" Then, the second related question is, "Do you have the desire to take on these kinds of risks?" You have to find that out, whatever niche market you're going into, and there's no use kidding these people that you have something that is a low-risk product. That's a little easier in our niche because our potential customer knows that if he has one hundred thousand bushels of corn out there in the bin, it's a high-risk product. I am not afraid to use the word "risk" when I'm talking to a prospect about futures and prices moving—he has a first-hand knowledge of how prices can move and the dollars and cents it means—but that's still part of what we have to do when we talk to him—assess his desire to accept risk.

Let's go back to seminars for a minute. You're always doing them. Any other advice?

Because of the numbers you have to deal with, you have to keep in perspective what you're trying to accomplish. If you go out there and say, "I'll try to do one seminar and see if I get enough business to justify it," that's not going to work. You have to do a whole series of seminars, and you have to adapt them as you do them so that you continue what works and you quit doing what doesn't work. *It's important to take a long-range viewpoint.* We've had people call us who attended a meeting five years ago. At that time they weren't interested in doing anything, but since then, they've discovered their attitude has changed, that maybe they need to take a different perspective. There are a lot of things that can happen over time. When you're planting seeds out there today, it's like planting an orchard. You're not going to harvest it next week.

Another way I look at a seminar is as prospect contact hours. To put it in a simpler fashion, if I have fifty people sitting in a room and I talk to them for two hours, I have one hundred prospect contact hours. If I do one a week, that's one hundred hours a week of prospect time I put in. I will venture to guess that that will put me way ahead of all the other brokers who are prospecting every night from six until ten, five nights a week. In addition to that, I will gain something because of the presence of other people there. Whether it is the sponsor who introduced me as someone intelligent, or whether another attendee in the room confirms to a second attendee that I must be worthwhile or the first guy wouldn't be there, I have some dynamics that are working in my favor that you don't have when you're on the telephone calling and taking the guy away from his TV show.

How would people in a larger market without ag connections get people to come to a seminar?

I think it's more difficult, and I say that because I don't have much experience in trying to do it. If I were to do that, I would try to become the expert in a particular niche in the market pertinent to that area. The way you do that is to supply information to people who are interested in it. Let's say you're wanting to get into the niche market of interest rate futures. I would figure out where I could go to meet the lenders who are inherently interested in interest rates: "What are interest rates going to do?" Maybe that would be breakfast clubs, maybe that would be the Kiwanis, the Rotary, the Lions—you'd have to do a little bit of research to find out where these people tend to do their social things—then I'd try to get in front of those groups. I would offer to come in and give a little noon-hour presentation about the impact of the Federal Reserve interest-rate tightening and the implication that has on shorter-term and longer-term interest rates. Whatever organizations they belong to are usually starved for speakers, so if you can come in and make a ten- or fifteen-minute presentation and leave some written material with the people, you create your own expertise. You become an expert in their eyes, as long as you make your presentation in a fashion that adds to your credibility and doesn't detract from it. Understand when you're going there, you're not selling anything. You're offering information, you're offering your expertise. What's interesting is that bankers move—they're always moving to different banks. So, if you stay in contact with particular individuals, you build an automatic network; in five years, probably half of those guys have gone to different banks.

People remember you five years later? How are you well known? Advertising? Publicity?

One of the blessings that has occurred in my life was my being asked to be an analyst on *Market to Market*, a nationally syndicated show on public broadcasting. I've been doing that since 1978, and that's a real help. It allows me to maintain a presence in front of people. Also, I've been in the same town (Perry, Iowa) since 1979, and I've had the same incoming WATS number since 1979. So any of the business cards we've distributed during that time has the right phone number on it.

You mentioned that you were lucky enough to be an analyst

on *Market to Market.* **It's not just luck. How did you put yourself in a position to be asked to do that?**

It was more luck than anything else. A neighbor of mine named George Mills, a well-known historian in Iowa, worked on a project with Dan Miller, who was the executive producer of *Market to Market,* and George put in a plug for me. So I was asked, along with some others, to appear on a semi-rotating basis. I've been there ever since. Now once again though, if I were not in that spot, I'd try to get myself into that spot. I would approach the local media, and it's a lot easier to start with radio. As an example, let's say your specialty was financial futures. Gosh, if you could have figured out a way to explain derivatives in 1994, there was such a niche out there. If you can make it simple enough that a junior high kid can understand what a derivative is and how it works, I would think you could become known as the expert in a particular market place relatively quickly.

What about cold calls?

Tell him exactly what you're doing. You're calling him, and you've got to have a reason for calling. Every time you call the guy, you've got to have a reason for calling.

So what is the reason?

If I were to do cold calls—I'm not in the business of doing that— but if I were to do that, I'd call to make an appointment.

But why would the guy want to give you an appointment?

The first thing is to qualify. "I see that you're an owner of a metal-processing company, and I realize that many times the movements in some of the commodity markets have an impact on what you're paying for your products or what you're selling your products for. The reason for my call today is to see whether I could talk to you about helping you with better pricing of your inputs or better pricing of your outputs." Then be quiet and let him talk. You're really just trying to find out answers to your questions and the more they're talking, the more answers you'll get. The more you're talking, the more time is going by that you're not finding out information. You've got to do the legwork. There's no substitute, and it's not going to give you a lot of immediate results. That's what you do on weekends.

What about weekends?

What I'm really saying is, a marketing effort has to take place. Some of that your firm may well have done, but if your firm isn't doing it for you, you have to do it for yourself.

What would be some examples of that?

Spend a Saturday doing some letters that go to the various organizations attended by the people you want to use as your niche; e.g., Kiwanis, Rotary, etc. Prepare reports that can be faxed to the newspapers in the area where you want to do your marketing. Then, every week there's something from you that goes out to each one of those newspapers. Sooner or later, when they have a blank space, they're going to stick your article in there. Maybe you try to get next to the radio people, so that they call you and interview you, or you give them a tape, or you give them marketing reports or something. In this way, you spend the weekends doing marketing for your business. Most of it's going to be written material so that it's taken care of. That way you don't have to worry about that the rest of the week.

You've touched on a lot, but I have another question: advice

to brokers in general. If I sent my son to you, what advice would you have?

There are several very good parts to this business. Better talk about the good before the bad, huh? You can control your income better in this industry than any other industry. I've seen people in this business who have been total failures and I've seen people who are multi-millionaires. You can be anywhere in between. A lot has to do with how hard you work and how smart you work. So, as the Chicago Mercantile Exchange tape program says, "You are the master of your destiny." I don't know of any other industry that has that capability. It's also an exciting industry because you're right on the edge of the news all the time. It's amazing the number of times you read an article in a newspaper, and you've already seen it on the news wire the day before. Or you see an article in the newspaper and they really get it out-of-whack with reality. You really are on the cutting edge, and I think it's an industry that's going to continue being a strong one in the years ahead.

It was interesting when I talked to my father about getting out of the telephone company and going into the futures business. He was pretty cautious because he thought there would always be a telephone company. What's interesting is that the telephone company, in this twenty-some years I've been away from it, has completely changed. A lot of people who thought they would always have a secure job, didn't, what with competition, the other long-distance carriers, etc. The futures business, however, has turned out to have had greater growth than the particular spot where I was in the telephone business. So there are those pluses. There are also the things you learn as far as working with people and markets and sales and so forth. Even if you're not successful in this business, you can carry a lot with you the rest of your life. You learn a lot of things that may give you some indication of where you should go, and I think that would be a plus, even if you don't happen to be successful as a broker.

Let me shift over to the negative side. The negative side to this business is that it's very stressful. The fact of the matter is that you will never figure out what the markets are going to do. You can work as hard as you possibly can trying to figure out the markets and initiate a trade, and it'll be wrong. Sometimes you'll just luckily put on a trade and it'll turn out to be right. So you can do the very best job that you know how to do, and then immediately have the market smack you up beside the head and tell you you're wrong. You have to be able to deal with failure and you have to be able to deal with the results of a bad trade when you're talking with a customer. You also have to have some particularly strong money-management skills because there will be people who will tell you a check's in the mail, and it will never get there. You have to stand the risk of that customer you're working with. We can try in every way possible to reduce that risk, but the fact of the matter is, somebody's going to catch you.

You also will make errors in the business. You'll write on the wrong side of the order pad and before you've figured it out, it'll have cost you money—and it might be an awfully lot of money. You've got to be able to recover from those kinds of setbacks. Sometimes people will go along and everything will be going just hunky-dory, and all of a sudden a series of setbacks will hit them— it's not a question of *whether* it will hit them but *when*—and some of them fold and never recover. So it takes a pretty strong constitution to do this business; not everybody is cut out to do it. I would say that it's the minority of people who are. It's a particularly challenging business. As a consequence, on the flip side of that, if you're successful, it's a pretty good paying business.

How can someone decide if this business is for them? Let's say they've been in it a couple years and they're still not sure?

My guess is, if they've been in it for a couple years and they're still not sure, they need to put together a really specific plan for the third year. Say to yourself, "This is what I'm going to accomplish in this third year," and it needs to have a commitment from a standpoint of time, and it needs to have an aggressive allocation of that time among the various parts of this business: marketing, sales, and trading. These allocations have to be the kinds of allocations that will result in increased business. Then there's satisfaction in your own life of doing the business that's commensurate with your level of income. I don't know quite how to say that, but I really think that if, after that third year, you've done those things that you promised yourself you were going to do, and you're still wondering, it's probably time to look for something different to do. *This is tough business to do if you don't like it.*

What are the traits of the successful brokers you've seen?

They've got to be hard workers, and at the same time they've got to be smart workers. They have to not take things too personally, have to be able to let it roll off. A friend of mine once said that you have to be like a duck. You've got to let everything roll off your back. Don't let it soak in.

There's no room in this business for people who are even a little bit dishonest. That'll come back to haunt them. Honesty and integrity are very important traits. They have to have empathy with their customers, they have to understand where their customers are coming from.

You've also got to be more like a willow tree and less like an oak because the wind's going to blow north, then it's going to blow south, then it's going to blow north, and if you are a person with a strong opinion, if you're unable to change your mind quickly, it's going to be a difficult business. You've got to be able to change your mind quickly, and get on the other side of the market.

Brokers have said to me, "I'm working hard, nothing is happening." How can they tell if they're just spinning their wheels?

There're a few things you can control. *One is, "How many people did I talk to today who are new prospects?"* Non-customers and real potential prospects. Around here, we try to hit twenty. It's a son-of-a-gun to hit twenty, but if you hit twenty a day, five days a week, one hundred a week, you end up with, under our norms, five customers.

How can a broker tell if he's working smart in addition to hard?

Did you make the calls? That's the hard part. What were the results? That's the smart part. If he made those one hundred phone calls in a week, and at the end of the week, he's got nothing that's headed toward opening business, then he'd better go back and look at where he got those hundred names.

How do you know it's the names as opposed to you?

That's a very good question. In our situation here, if somebody's made those calls, and we don't look at them quite as one hundred, we'll sure look at it at the end of the month. If they haven't had any success with the names we've generated, if they haven't gotten any business, then I'm going to presume it's the broker. If a broker is doing this all alone, he or she has to go to someone for counsel, presumably the office manager. If not the manager, then to some other person in the industry who is a mentor. Have that person listen in on some telephone calls, see how it's going, critique the calls and make some suggestions.

John, do you talk about business with your wife?

You're bringing up something that's really important. One of the detrimental things I see commodity brokers doing is not sharing their experiences at home. They go home and the market just went limit against them. All their customers are in, and the market's limit against them. They might have just blown somebody out of the market who didn't have enough margin; there's a debit in the account and the guy already told you he's not going to pay you. So you go home, thinking, "Not only do I not have the capacity to earn money, but they're going to be taking extra money out of my check for the debit, and I don't know where I'm going to find new customers because I just took the guts out of half the customers I've got. I know they're all mad at me. I haven't talked to them all, but I know they're all mad at me." Now you go home, and your wife comes home, or is at home, and says, "How was your day?" Now, the guy's tendency is to want to spare the woman all the pain and the details, and unfortunately, the woman thinks he's mad at her. Instead of saying, "The market got me today," he becomes quiet and withdrawn. The woman immediately assumes there's something wrong in the relationship between the husband and the wife, when in reality it was just, "The market got me." All they have to do is come home and say, "Boy, the market got me today. It went limit against me, and I don't even want to go in tomorrow. I made thirty margin calls today," and on and on. Just go ahead and dump it out and get it over because otherwise, the wife is going to assume that their relationship is the reason for his attitude. That's a normal assumption.

Are there any books, tapes, or courses you'd recommend?

Dale Carnegie's excellent. I would strongly recommend a Dale Carnegie course, probably above all the others that I have been around. I like to listen to tapes, all kinds of motivational tapes, that teach you how to sell. A big part of sales will be your own innate ability to be curious enough to ask the questions to find out what the needs and problems are. But there are various techniques for learning how to ask those questions better and motivational assistance to keep you asking those questions, rather than quitting.

Where can they go for this kind of sales material?

Talk to somebody you respect who sells insurance. They have a tremendous wealth of sales assistance, better than the commodity business.

John, how about the importance of self-esteem?

Self-esteem is certainly important in any business, but particularly important in the sales business because most of the people we talk to are going to say, "no." If you accept that as a, "No, I don't like you, and you're not a good person, and you're not the kind of person I want to talk to," and all those other kinds of things that can pull your esteem down, it's very difficult to make the next phone call. So you have to have enough self-esteem that you don't lose the optimism in your voice when you call the next person.

How can someone improve his self-esteem, self-confidence, or self-respect?

Have some successes. Set some goals that you can accomplish. In the case of this business, you can set a goal every day of the number of people you're going to call. Don't set goals that depend on something you have no control over.

If you have real problems with self-esteem, find a good counselor. Find somebody you can talk to.

How about the psychological health of customers? I've heard it said some customers are adrenaline junkies.

When you look over a whole list of customers, there are some people who consider a one-thousand-dollar trading profit or loss totally insignificant, no big deal. For other people, a one-thousand-dollar win or loss is tremendously exciting or depressing. The problem is not if the person has no excitement making a one-thousand-dollar profit. The problem is if a person has no excitement making a one-hundred-thousand or five-hundred-thousand or one-million dollar profit. The point I'm trying to make here is that for those people who are "adrenaline junkies," there's never a win that's great enough, and there's never a loss that's bad enough to get them to change their ways. Of course, there's nothing wrong with letting the winner run, but those same people have a real problem cutting the losers short.

So how do you handle them?

Get away from them, or understand that you are playing hot potato with that particular customer and don't let them burn you. Be particularly tough on them. Tell your manager and your margin people this is a problem situation. Double or triple the margins, shift to inter-day wire transfers, don't let them catch you. Unfortunately, these people will tend to become a big portion of your business, so you'll be sitting there with one person controlling thirty to forty percent of your business, and pretty soon that one person is controlling you. Then you might do something that's stupid—you don't enforce the margin policies, you don't run your business exactly the way you should run your business.

That person can cost you the most, and as an employer of brokers, if I have a broker that is that kind of person, sooner or later, I'm going to have a problem.

Can you think of any traits of those who don't make it in this business?

Biggest problem I see in bad brokers is that they become like kamikaze pilots in a bad trade. They go down in flames because they can't say 'enough is enough' and get out. They don't have money management skills, so in every trade they risk the entire business of a customer.

Any advice for struggling brokers who used to be successful? How do they get back on track?

Be a mentor. Start with a brand new broker and help that broker build his or her business. It'll get you back to the ABCs of doing the business. I think that's the best advice I have. It's always interesting to me when I bring a new person into my office who doesn't know anything. He or she can go through and get more out of a stack of prospects than an experienced person because the experienced person doesn't see anything in that stack of prospects. The inexperienced one doesn't know any better. The inexperienced person calls them all, treats them all like they're potential customers, asks all the questions, dots all the i's, crosses all the t's, and sure enough, there are a few people in there who want to do business.

When you send prospects the papers, what percent come back?

We bat five hundred. Half of the account forms we send out come back in. We make sure we call the people we've sent forms to. Once again we go back to our customer-management system. When we send out papers, we're going to call that person in three or four days, and we'll try to get them to fill out the papers over the telephone. "Let me just walk you through this." Because everybody's busy and everybody puts off those things that don't seem urgent. Heaven only knows, these forms are thick enough and full of enough risk words that sometimes people will open the form and say, "Well, I think I'll pass on this," and set it aside. So we call them up and walk them through the forms, or we'll go out and sit down and visit with them and have them fill out the forms. We'll invite them in, we'll meet them half way. We do a lot of different things to get the paperwork taken care of.

Are there any red flags as far as clients to stay away from, clients who might potentially take advantage of you?

The only thing I can say to brokers about this is "Go with your gut instinct." In this business, you have to follow your gut instinct. If in your stomach you feel there's going to be a problem with a customer, treat it as if there is a problem. The second thing is, don't just keep it to yourself and don't just take it to someone else who works with you. Take it one step higher. Take it to the manager, take it to the margin person, take it to someone who can offer a more neutral view, who will talk to you from a more neutral posture.

John, what advice do you wish you would have had when you started in this business?

I wish someone would've told me who was going to be the very best money manager, and I simply would have been his fund-raiser and let him trade, and I'd be hopefully sitting on a beach somewhere.

What about managed money in our industry?

Well, it's obviously a big growth area of the business and is liable to continue to be a growth area of the business, as I see it. We have spent very little time trying to do managed money business or discretionary-type business, and I wish I would have invested some effort and some dollars in that years ago. If I were coming into it again, I think I would look at this business very hard as to where would my niche be. Would it be in the transactional business or in the managed side of the business? Depending on how brokers want to spend their days, it may well be that there are people out there who are much better suited to raising funds for managed business than for raising funds for transactional business. I've heard it said there are the hunters, gatherers, and then there's the other side, the people who trade. If you get next to a good trading advisor, this business can become more like an annuity, whereas if you're a transactional broker, there's very little of that. You're having to continually generate new business.

Any other advice that you wish you would have had to make your life as a futures broker easier?

It would be nice to get good experience, good training in the actual trading, in the determining of commodity trades. I don't know, I'm talking based on things that I've read, but if someone such as a Richard Dennis takes you under his wing and says "Look, I'm going to teach you how to trade commodities," that would be a tremendous assistance. If you could find someone who is a very good trader, do whatever is necessary in order to learn how to trade, and then put that together with your sales experience. If you have the gift to be able to do that kind of trading, you don't need to worry about the sales, somebody else will bring the money to you. So find out which one of those directions is the right one for you.

What about stress?

Well, as I said earlier, the stress in this business is real. It's probably one of the largest reasons people fail in this business.

How do you handle stress?

Don't take yourself too seriously. Don't take the business too seriously. It's only money. Walk away from the business when you go home at night and forget about it the best you can. I see people in this business who don't want to take vacations. That's a big mistake.

How about setting goals?

I'm not very good at that. I should be better. I go for very short-term ones.

What kind of short-term goals should young brokers have?

"How many calls did you make today?" I've got to keep coming back to this, and by a call, how did you define the call? Define the call as talking to the person who makes the decision and moving the process one notch closer toward doing business or removing a prospect. Do it on a daily basis.

How about the importance of listening?

Well, listening is the biggest part of communicating with prospects, clients, and fellow workers. It's something I have to work on because it's not something I do naturally. I have to try to zip my lip and listen. I hope one of these years I'll get better at it.

What advice would you give to younger brokers on how to improve their listening skills? Why should they?

Well, the reason they should is because that's when you will learn *everything*. Keep your mouth closed and your ears open. You can't sell something until you've learned enough about the prospect to have your product solve their problem.

How do you do it?

You've just got to think about it. "I'd appreciate your input." Great little saying. Then stop. Listen. Ask a question, a wide open question, and then be quiet again. See? You may have to do some reading, you may have to listen to some tapes, you may have to go to Dale Carnegie. *Your prospects and customers like you best when **they** are doing the talking.* When you're on the telephone, ask an open-ended question, not a question they can simply answer "yes" or "no." Then count to about five, and if you think he's just thinking, count to ten. Get yourself some little techniques to help you accomplish what it is your trying to accomplish from a listening standpoint.

How about attitude?

Well, attitude is probably the most important thing. When you get up in the morning, do you get up with an attitude of, "Boy, things are not going to go well today, things are bad, the glass is half-empty." If that's the kind of person you are, then you're probably in the wrong business. *You've got to have a positive attitude because nobody wants to talk to a person with a negative attitude.* Your customers and prospects need to recognize you as a positive, upbeat, fun-to-be-around kind of person. If you're not naturally that kind of person, you're going to have to work extra hard on that aspect of your personality.

Compliance?

The right approach to compliance in our opinion is, never get in the gray area. It's either white or it's black. If it's black, you're not doing it; if it's white, you are doing it. Always stay well inside of the boundary.

You refer to your niche. Is that something young brokers need to do, become specialists, or can they be generalists?

I think it would be awfully difficult to be considered a knowledgeable person or somewhat of an expert on a whole range of different topics because there's just way too much stuff out there, too many different kinds of commodities and too many different aspects of each commodity to try to stay on top of it all. If you're going to be a generalist, you're going to need to be selling someone else as well, such as being an equity raiser for a trading manager. You'd talk about commodities and the industry and the concept in general, while someone else actually calls the shots and executes trades.

Any war stories? Good or bad?

I can think of all kinds of war stories. I might talk about one customer. We had one group we talked with for a period of years, and we basically traded information back and forth. We knew they did some sizeable futures business, but we never really figured we had much of a shot at it. Still, we were tickled to share information back and forth, and to even have these people talk to us. You know, when somebody pretty important comes along and wants to talk to you, it makes you feel good. So we were in that process for several years, then kind of lightly asked for some business and were able to get a significant piece of business. We found the reason we were able to do that business was because our perspective was different from other brokers they were talking with. We had the unique advantage of being located in Perry, Iowa which we had thought might be a disadvantage. For that particular customer, our location turned out to be an advantage because we didn't have the same viewpoint as the "Chicago brokers." There was one of those interesting situations where it turned out something we had thought was a bit of a liability was an asset. Also, sometimes you just don't know how long you need to prospect before you can land some business. We were prospecting, although we didn't really consider it prospecting.

I don't know if you'd consider it a war story, but another thing we do in our office is, we swap customers around. We realize that personalities are all different. Each customer has his own personality, the broker has his own personality. For example, I tried hard to handle one particular customer, and I just wasn't able to do so. We had very different personalties. Then Mike Smith started working with that customer and has done an absolutely outstanding job. *So sometimes you have to be willing to give up something for the benefit of the whole.* We've always had the approach here that if a customer doesn't seem happy, we strongly consider switching brokers for that customer.

Personal visits. Any advice about what should happen on a personal visit?

Try to be like your customer. If your customer is dressed in a suit, be in a suit. If your customer is dressed in blue jeans, be in blue jeans, maybe just a little nicer blue jeans than the customer has. Be very respectful of their time, they're busy. They don't have all day to spend with you. You're there to try to get to know them, and you need to be careful about expressing your opinions if they're not widely held by other people. If when you drive up, you see a *Vote for Clinton* sticker on the back of his car, don't tell him about the Rush Limbaugh show you were listening to, unless you do it making fun of Limbaugh. You have to be aware of the other person's point of view and don't run diametrically opposed to it. I'm not saying that you have to acquiesce to the point that all your opinions are the same as the other person's opinions, but you have to be aware of the other person's opinions and values, and don't overtly run counter to them.

Anything else that should happen in personal meetings?

Sure, find out what their interests are in your market areas, in something that's commodity related. Also find out what their hobbies are. You need to have some basis for your conversation other than the commodity business. Does he have a family? How old are his kids? What's his wife do?

Also, if you look in the prospect's office, find an area of interest based on what's hanging on the walls; you have a common area for discussion that is totally nonthreatening and enjoyable to the prospect. So if you see something that is golf related in his office, you can always talk about golf and perhaps arrange a time later when you can get together and play golf. Or if there is some other kind of hobby or activity showing up in his office, you can key off it very quickly and you can have a nonthreatening conversation and can make a friend. Bear in mind that's the bottom line. You're trying to make a friend when you go in there, and the best way to make a friend, whether it be in a business conversation or in a social setting, is to find some common area of discussion.

How do you recommend servicing an account?

I'd ask the account. You can ask in a nonthreatening fashion, and it's best to ask right off the bat. Say, *"You know, I'd like to be a broker who takes care of all your needs, but I don't want to be somebody who badgers you. And I have some customers who like me to call them three times a day and I have some customers*

who like me to call them once a month. Where would you put
yourself in that spectrum?" I tell my customers I use a contact
management system on my computer and that I'm going to put
them in my computer to be called in so many days.

Anything else about servicing an account?

The other criterion is "How frequently do you want to be called,
and when do you want to be called from the standpoint of events?"
Same kind of situation, when that event occurs, even if it's just
the afternoon of the morning you talked to him, call them up and
say, "I put a note in here that when the corn got down to $2.49 I
was supposed to give you a call. It just traded $2.49¼ and I
thought I'd better call you." If you simply say it in that fashion
and then be quiet, the customer will tell you if he is interested or
not interested or, "Thanks I appreciate the call." Take your cue
from what he says next.

　　　Also, I like to send money out of an account. Let's say, as
an example, a customer tells me they're going to be trading a
couple of contracts at a time. So I'll ask them to send in three
thousand dollars to cover a couple of contracts of grain. Then
let's say we go down the road three or four months: they've traded
a couple of contracts of grain and they've been profitable and
they've now got five thousand dollars in their account. I will call
them up and say, "You know, we've been trading a couple of
contracts of grain and it really only takes two to three thousand
dollars to do that, I'm going to send out two thousand, and that
check will leave Chicago today." Sometimes they'll say, "Oh no,
don't bother," but they always appreciate that I'm calling them
and telling them I'm sending some money out. *On the flip side of*
that, we try to call customers the first day they have a margin call
because at that point the customers can make up their minds as
to whether they want to stay in the position or get out of it while
the loss is not too large. If you wait until the third or fourth day,
invariably the loss will become larger, and suddenly they'll make

a decision that's based on faulty reasoning such as, "I can't take a loss that big." So if they can't take a loss that big, that means they'll hang on to it, and Murphy's Law is that it will always get bigger. So call them on the first day.

Something else we do that we think is a real customer-service plus is that if we don't get a hold of the customers on the phone, we send them a note. "Tried to call you today, missed you, give me a call when you have a chance." People seem to like that. Of course, we do the same thing on margin calls while we keep trying to reach him by phone. We do the same thing on positions. We try to call him and report a fill—we always report all fills—and we also report all unables. The reason is that sometimes customers think they bought something, and then, when the market goes up a bunch, they find out it wasn't bought. They never knew that. They assumed it was bought, and now they are mad at you because they didn't know they weren't in. So send them a note if you can't get them on the phone. Fax machines are wonderful for that.

Do you leave messages on answering machines?

I certainly do. I not only leave a message, I tell the customers everything I wanted to tell them in person on the machine. So I'll give them one or two minutes of whatever I want them to hear. Much better off for the machine to relay it than for a child or a spouse to relay it. I'd much rather catch the machine. I hear some brokers say they don't like machines. I even had a stock-broker call one time and say some stuff on my answering machine that scared my wife. I called him the next day and asked the reason he did that. He said it was because he hated those answering machines. I closed my account that day. I have an answering machine at my house because it is a tool I use in my day-to-day business. You can either be willing to use my tool, or you can decide not to use my tool. If you don't use my tool, I probably won't do much business with you.

Anything else about servicing accounts?

Remember the account is your best source of new business. To the degree this account is the kind of account you want, cultivate that account and that account's friends. Go to the birthday party, go to the men's stag at the golf course. Do all the various things you can do to not only do business with that particular customer, but with others in the same group.

John, in closing, is there anything you'd like to add? Do you have a personal philosophy about our business?

To me this business is a craft or a skill, the same as many other crafts or skills. You can't really learn it in books. This book may help, but you have to get out and do it. You can get help and ideas and so forth, but ideally, you need to have someone take you on as an apprentice. Somebody who teaches you how to do the business, encourages you when you're down, knocks you down a little bit when you're cocky, chides you to make those additional phone calls, and listens to the phone calls and says, "Gees, if you'd just done this a little differently, that a little differently or try this or try that. I think this is something that's pulling you down, here." Those are the things we need to have when we're learning a craft, and it's not taught anywhere else. So I think most successful people in this business will go back to someone who took them by the hand and guided them through some rough spots, and everybody needs that. You can't do it all by yourself. So if you're going to get into this business, look for a manager, mentor, trainer, or person to help guide you. That's what the people in this book are trying to do: help you. Be open. You've got to be open. You've got to be willing to try new and different things and you have to be willing to be very flexible. Have fun while you're doing it, laugh, and be around people who are happy.

Roy S. (Bucky) Sheffield

PaineWebber Incorporated
Portland, Oregon

What's your background, Bucky?

Born and raised in Lubbock, Texas. Majored in political science
and history at Texas Tech, graduated in 1974. This was about the
time the Russians really started buying U.S. grain. Since Lubbock was and is an ag area, people there had a lot more interest in
the price of wheat, corn, and cotton than they had in the price of
General Motors, IBM, or AT&T. So, having grown up in an ag
area and having a background in economics, commodities was
just a natural area for me to go into. Got into this business right
after college. Boy, that was a long time ago. Moved to Portland
in 1982 to manage the commodity office of a major firm and have
been here ever since.

Do you remember how you got your first few accounts?

Friends of my family were my first few accounts. We had big livestock and cotton markets in the mid- to late seventies which we traded. My beginning was basically in the farm community, farmers mainly, people who were involved in agriculture. I did some business with a few country elevators in and around Lubbock when I first began. It was pretty difficult to get started in a commercial or a hedge kind of situation back then. So my entry was almost one hundred percent individuals, and now it's almost one hundred percent companies, corporations.

How did you make the switch?

Well, when I came to Portland, the office had a very strong cash grain background, cash wheat in particular. The PNW, that's the Pacific Northwest, is a strategic area for world wheat trade. The majority, maybe ninety percent, of U.S. wheat that goes to Korea, Japan, Pakistan, Egypt, comes out of the PNW. Cash wheat was basically the backbone of the office when I got here, and most of the clients, therefore, were companies, not individuals. That's how I got into companies, into corporations. I was lucky, I inherited it.

Do you have a particular approach to trading?

I'm about seventy-five percent fundamental, but twenty-five percent technical because I don't think anyone can trade intelligently without being aware of the direction of the market. Not only moving averages, but the whole technical picture is very important. When it comes to our specialty, wheat, the amount of high-quality fundamental research done here in the States is very limited. That's partly why someone like myself can create a little niche in the cash wheat and futures business. Very little quantitative analysis is done. I'm a client of an analyst in Washington, D.C., Andy Bellingham, whom I've known for a number of years. He's a soybean and grain person. Andy puts out very thorough analytical data which a number of people not only in the States, but around the world subscribe to. Rumors don't appeal. News flashes don't appeal. Most of the typical information coming off the news wire doesn't appeal to the big players in any part of the cash or futures business. It's much too shallow. You have to go way beyond that if you want to really help them. That's what it takes to be really successful in our business: really helping your customers. It's called "value-added."

Another thing that's really helped me is that I just trade wheat. Now, I'm surely not claiming to be smarter than anyone else, but I do think that when you trade only one market, it makes you a lot more adept when you go into a group of sophisticated people in that area. You can talk from in-depth experience and for an extended time with facts about the potential and parameters of the market. When you have the ability to talk about a market, people feel comfortable, feel that you're aware of all aspects of that market. You can't intelligently talk about a market if all you can say is, "Well, we're in an up-trend," or "Here's the moving average," or "The open interest or the carry-over is that." This is not the kind of information that gives clients a great deal of comfort if they're committing millions and millions of dollars to a cash or futures position.

Where do you get your information? Where does a typical broker go for good, in-depth information beyond the ordinary?

You have to develop relationships with people who trade that cash commodity or underlying futures. You obviously can't get in immediately with the people who are major traders; none of us can, but you must develop a dialogue with people who spend their day trading that particular commodity. That's their business.

How can one do that?

Start small. Now, what you do with these relationships once you're given the opportunity will demonstrate how you flourish and how you build and grow. It still goes back to the concept that you have to provide useful information and sound advice to people.

A while back you mentioned value-added. What are some examples of value-added?

One example is something I mentioned before. Value-added is bringing to the party information that is not widely disseminated over the news wires or not easily gained. It's information that's available if people are smart enough to get it or willing enough to dig for it. I'm not talking about any sort of inside information; however, these are things our clients couldn't find on the news wire. They are very interested because they're trying to compete with different origins for the same customers. I think that's value-added. Another value-added service is to be able to talk to clients about a particular market. I have two clients with whom I have weekly conference calls. We talk about market conditions, both in their areas—they're international clients—and in the States, how it all relates to them, where we see the markets today, where we think they're going.

So these are three people on the phone, you and two clients?

No, two different conference calls. We do that a couple times a week. I think you have to be able to talk about markets, but the more adept you become in understanding what moves markets, the more you're able to listen. It's my opinion that the longer you are in this business, *the more correct decisions you make by listening than by dictating.* It's been my experience, John, that people who trade have enormous egos, and those egos many times are probably their worst enemies. They think they're smarter. They think they're quicker. You develop the ability to sit back and listen to what each customer is saying, what your research tells you, what your experience tells you, the whole gamut, then put it all together, you usually get a pretty decent idea of what a particular situation is like. You can't do it if you don't listen. *If you don't listen, you're missing a good, easy chance to learn.* Most insecure brokers don't listen very well. They think they always have to prove how smart they are.

One of the complaints we get in our surveys is that the broker didn't listen. Any tips on how to listen?

I think a lot of it is the ego thing. Ego has a way of becoming antagonistic. Many people, looking at someone who tries to force his ideas or his values on them, develop a certain antagonism towards them. I might not admit it, but it makes it a heck of a lot easier for my prospect to call Fred than to call Bucky if he feels that antagonism towards me or from me.

If I have six or eight very important clients who are very influential not only in the States but also in world trade, I'm a lot better off listening to what they have to say and what their situation is. They bring me something I obviously don't have access to otherwise. That's probably the most important thing any trader can have. There are a number of brokers in similar positions. *If you value what your customers are telling you, if you do your homework, if you keep your ego out of it, you won't feel compelled to do all the talking.* You'll have a better chance of being a good listener. If you're a good listener, you'll stand out from the crowd. *Don't you tend to like quiet people? Try to be one.*

Bucky, any one reason for your success?

John, I would say if I've had any success it's because I have a great group of clients who trade with me.

But you had to get those clients and you had to service them right.

I did, but I still think it goes back to giving people the right information. Now, I have some clients who basically only call me—I answer the phone and turn the orders in—but they're few and far between. Clients have to feel like they need you and that you bring something to the party they don't get from anyone else.

Bucky, any comments on money management as it pertains to trading?

If I say anything, I'd say trade less rather than more. It's as if someone said, "Your life depends on making money this year trading any market." You have to have a credit at the end of the year. It's a whole lot easier to have a credit at the end of the year if you make three or four trades than it is if you make three or four hundred. That's my opinion. That doesn't mean you get a loser and you stay with it forever, but when you get it right, don't ever get out. *There's an old saying that there's more money to be made sitting than trading, and I think there's a lot of truth to that.*

Any advice about prospecting?

You have to define what kind of clients you're trying to get. Are you interested in people who are willing to take more risk on a certain percent of their investments? Do you want people who are involved in the cash side, or in the daily activity of a cash trader? If you're starting with speculators, you must approach people and make sure they can afford to lose the money they're putting into commodities. Then you define how much money they're willing to risk and trade with that amount in mind, not a penny more. *I personally think you're better off not selling a particular trade.* Also, tell your clients and prospects, *"anybody can handle profits, we're concerned with losses,"* and go from there. You must also explain to people they need to accept the fact that they're going to have price swings with their money. Certain people don't want price swings. Futures trading is obviously not for them. Others have a certain amount of money they feel comfortable seeing fluctuate.

What if somebody asks, "What's your minimum account size?"

Well, I'd ask them questions first. Get to know them a little. Check their temperament. *Maybe they shouldn't be trading no matter how much risk capital they have.* Depends on what they want, their needs, their tolerance for risk. Find out. Ask questions. If everything's go, I still would say hold it to five or ten percent of your liquid net worth. You know the old investment triangle. Emergency savings across the bottom, then house and college funds, insurance, and finally spec investments in the little area at the top. You need to limit how much you're going to risk to that five or ten percent. Then you have to keep their investment in shape, do the things that will make it last longer. If you're a broker and you're getting commissions from that account, obviously if that account goes kaboosh, there go your commissions. If your guy does well, you're going to do well. If the guy's got a ten thousand dollar account and you build it up to a hundred thousand, he's going to go from trading ones to fives which means you'll generate more revenue. I can't emphasize that enough, even though it's obvious: the more money you have to trade with, the more money you're going to make as a broker. The only way you get more money is either for clients to put more money in or to take it out of the market.

Let's say you want to go after wealthy individuals. Any advice on where to find them?

I haven't had any experience like that in a few years, but the people I saw who felt comfortable trading futures were people who were comfortable taking risks in other areas also. I grew up in Texas. People who are farmers obviously take big risks. People in the oil business obviously take big risks. People in real-estate development obviously take big risks. I think people who have risk in their professional area are more suited to accepting risk in general; they can adapt to the risk of trading commodity futures. It's very difficult to have an accountant sort of mentality and take it over to the futures market. Obviously there are people who have that mentality who do well trading, but in terms of finding individuals who feel comfortable with risk, I think they'd be more in that first category.

How about if brokers wanted to go after commercial business? How would they approach those markets?

You go to the prospects. Go to them, go see them. Obviously, if you're in New York, you're not going to see a lot of soybean producers or cattle feeders or whatever, but you have bankers, importers, or exporters who have to hedge currency risk. Back when we were in Texas soliciting commercial business, we'd go out to a feed yard and visit cattle feeders. You begin to develop a rapport, you do something for them. Maybe they have an idea that a certain customer of theirs would be interested in your services. *From a commercial standpoint, you have to go to the source. You have to go to them—they're not going to come to you.*

On going to people, what about telemarketing versus going to see folks or having them come see you?

Well, my feeling is you have to see people face-to-face. The majority of my overseas clients are in Australia. I go to Australia once a year, sometimes more. You can talk to somebody on the phone every day, but I think it's important for them to see your face and to press the flesh at least once a year.

Let's say that some people reading this chapter have come to the conclusion that they are not very good traders. Should they get out of the business? I heard you say that to succeed in this business you have to make money for your clients, and not many brokers seem to be able to do that consistently. Is there anything else they can do?

Well, obviously there have been many brokers who have been very successful giving money to other people to trade. But whether you trade it or somebody else trades it, keeping those clients, those relationships, still goes back to being profitable. Obviously, if you had a situation where you felt comfortable with someone else doing the things you were short in, such as trading, that would make a lot of sense. It doesn't mean you have to get out of the business if you can't trade well. I think it's a whole lot harder to be an expert trader than it is to be good with people. Yes, I'm sure there are brokers out there who are excellent traders who aren't very good with people, and there are brokers who are very good with people who can't trade very well. We all have our niches. *Do what you're good at and don't do what you're not good at.*

Bucky, any other prospecting advice?

When you talk with a prospect, if you sense they're just trying to take, rather than make it a give-and-take situation, that's a bad sign. If you can't sense give-and-take, then you're never going to have a very good relationship with that person. I didn't mention this earlier, but the relationship you have with a client has to be very special. It has to be very strong. It has to be built on honesty. You owe them honesty, and they in turn owe you the honesty of saying, "I don't intend to trade, I'm on the dole here," if that's the case. The best way to approach that is to be honest and say, "I have to be honest with you here, should I continue to talk with you with the intent of you opening an account and trading, or is this going to be an ongoing one-way situation?" In my experience, the easiest way to voice a concern is just to voice it, not to beat around the bush. Then you have an answer. Then you know how to go to the next step.

Anything else about honesty?

In my world, I don't think you can ever be successful without being completely honest with clients. If someone confides in you, that confidence always has to be respected. At the end of the day you'll be rewarded for it. Now, we do business with ten or twelve people who compete with each other many times. If they were all in a room together, would you say the same thing to one as you would to the other? You must be able to look yourself in the eye before you're able to look someone else straight in the eye. *Don't talk about other people's business.* Your prospects and clients will respect your honesty and they will confide in you more if they feel that you have the integrity that warrants their confidence.

Do you ever have to say to somebody, if they ask you a question, "I know the answer, but I'm not allowed to tell you." How do you handle that diplomatically?

Well, I guess I'm lucky. In all the years I've been trading out here, I've only had one person ask me a compromising sort of question and I said, "Let me give you that particular individual's number and you can call and ask him." I've been fortunate my clientele respect me enough to not put me in an awkward position.

What does servicing an account mean to you?

Provide the information the client asked for *and information he needs, even if he didn't ask for it.* For example, with a new individual spec account sometimes they don't even know which questions to ask. You have to ask the questions for them. This builds trust. This helps prevent surprises and problems. It goes back to what we talked about earlier. Listen to what they want from you and then give it accordingly. I think servicing an account is relating things that are very important to you and your client. It means executing their business in a timely and professional manner. We owe allegiance to our clientele to get the best possible fills, to get the quickest service, to do the things that get them the same kind of service as if they were right down there trading. I don't think just because you're a member of the Chicago Mercantile Exchange or the Chicago Board of Trade that you inherently do a better job or get better executions because you're standing there. I believe we pay the best people to do the best job they can for us on the floor. You have to make every effort to keep doing the best job you can. That's a pretty far-reaching task. So servicing an account to me is providing the things that they want and need . . . whether they know it or not.

Bucky, how do you handle the stress in this business? Is there any stress for you?

There is stress, no question about that. I handle it better at some times than I do at others. When you answer the phone to talk to someone, invariably you're going to be off in any market from time to time, dealing with the highs and the lows. If you're ecstatic when it's going well and morose when it's going badly, people don't want to be around that. They don't want to deal with that. You have to try to keep as level a demeanor as possible, and I think that's what being a professional means.

When people really get knocked down, do you have any advice for them on how to pick themselves up or how to come back?

To me, John, when you're going bad, the best way to get out of the dumps is to go back and look at the successes you've had. A lot of people keep a diary or journal of what they do every day. Go back and read what things you were doing when you were doing well, what successes you were having. You'll have them again. What you are today is not necessarily what you're going to be in the future. The markets definitely tell you that, and I think that's a good way to look at it. Maybe even go back and look at how big a bank account you had at that time. It will happen again. *The only people who can't come back from their failures are people who don't want to participate any more. As long as you want to participate, you have a chance to come back.*

What points should brokers cover during the first meeting with a client? How do you gain somebody's confidence or trust or respect?

You sell yourself. You sell what kind of person you are and what you're trying to accomplish by being involved with them. It's important to be straight up about this. Once you gain an audience with someone, you have to explain what you can bring to the party, what you hope to accomplish, what your goals are, and ask them if that fits what they're looking for. It's the same way with negotiating commissions. It has to work for both parties or it's never going to be any good over a period of time. If what you're bringing is not what they're looking for, say thank you very much, and go on from there. Also, if there is any element, any hint of distrust, if that's evident, you've got no chance.

But, in our surveys, some brokers are thought to be untrustworthy—why do you think that is?

If you want to have a relationship for a long time, you work with prospects and clients. Identify their needs, and maybe their needs at the time don't include trading, and therefore, no income for you right then. If you want to make x amount of dollars over the short term, so be it. In our industry, when people call up and sell special situations, I think it's very much like being a used car salesman. "Here, this is perfect for you. Buy it today, before someone else does." Often brokers have too many short-term objectives. "Well, let's see, I can call this guy and open the account, get x number of commissions out of him, and then I'll go get somebody else." You develop distrust, not only with yourself, but with the people whom you're soliciting when you're only trying to gain something short term. The clientele I have, I've traded with them for ten, fifteen years plus and hopefully I'll have a relationship with them for the next fifteen years. Approach it as, "I'm going to open this account and I'm going to have this account for x number of years, and we may not even trade that much." You can't be short term.

What written and mental goals should a broker have about equity raised? Do you believe in that?

No, I don't. I mean, is it good, are you doing well if you raise x number of dollars? What if you lose x number of dollars? Does that mean you're not doing well? That's a bad foundation to build on, but if you develop a strong relationship, it's going to be just as strong when you're doing well as when you're doing poorly.

If you don't have a relationship to begin with, it's really going to put the focus on the times you're going bad, and they leave. That's why people lose accounts. They don't have relationships, and the focus is on situations or trades.

How about sales training and sales techniques? Have you ever taken any sales courses?

No, but that's what we are, we're sales people. How does somebody get better at that? *It all goes back to listening, asking what you can do for someone, rather than telling them what you're going to do for them.* Once you listen, you accept the fact that what you have is not going to be appropriate for everyone you talk to. You have to be able to let go if you aren't the one.

Of the brokers you've seen, can you think of a few traits of the successful brokers?

They want to be successful in making money for their clients whether they do the trading or someone else calls the shots. That's their drive to do well. The days of sitting at your desk having the phone ring off the hook with people having their own trading ideas who want to trade through you are over. *If you're just an order taker, you're going to be paid like an order taker.* All the brokers I've seen do really well add value. That could be providing information, trading expertise, execution, availability. All of those things kind of tie together. Also, all the consistently successful people I've seen have had the futures business as one hundred percent of their driving force. That doesn't mean you can't have a family, it doesn't mean you can't have fun on the side, but the business itself really does have to be your driving force. I don't want to say you have to be obsessed with it, but it does have to be more important than going to work at nine and going home at five. I think you can have your family first, some people would say God, but I think you can have your family first and then your job, your trading, being a broker, has to come second. It has to come above your golf and your family vacations. It has to have a solid place. I've never seen anybody successful who goes on long vacations, unless somebody else is trading for them. I've never seen anybody successful who regularly leaves at one in the afternoon. I've never seen anybody successful who comes in fifteen minutes before the opening. You have to pay your dues. You have to put in the effort. Look at your clients. My clients trade. They are at risk, they come to work, stay until five o'clock or whatever it takes. You owe them that same effort, and I think that effort, whether you're a resource for information, tracking down a cash trade, tracking down a sale that was made to a different country, you have to be a resource to them. They have to feel they can call you for that information when the market's open, closed, and even nights and weekends when necessary. You have to be there all the time. Period. The other thing is, John, there aren't many people who do that out there. You have to be professional the whole way. Otherwise, you go back to that deal where you're sitting back waiting for somebody to bring something to you because you can't bring anything to them.

Can you see any trends in our business that are affecting or will affect brokers in our business?

The first thing is, there is tremendous opportunity for young brokers who are willing to do the right things and present themselves in a professional manner, gaining the respect of clients. Develop those sorts of talents, and you'll be appealing to a number of clients. The second thing is, we won't continue to see business discounted to the point where there's no reason to be in it. People used to want to be members of the exchanges so they could get member rates. Now, Joe Schmoe off the street can get rates almost like that. Ours can't continue to be a viable business when rates are discounted to where no one wants to participate. So I think that has to change.

What's a typical work day like for you?

I get up at about five in the morning, and I go to an athletic club where I ride a stationary bike, work out until about six-fifteen, five days a week. I take a shower, get down to the office between six-thirty and six-forty-five. I have an assistant who's in the office at five o'clock because of the currencies—those markets open at five-twenty-five. We don't have anybody who trades them, but we're open. Our markets are open from seven-thirty until eleven-fifteen. Then I go to lunch until about one. Then I'm in the office from one until five-thirty. I have two conference calls I make in the evening twice a week, from six-thirty until seven-fifteen from my home. We talk about the wheat market.

Do you have any war stories, good or bad, that the readers might learn from?

Anyone who trades markets is going to be in a position from time to time where they can't seem to do anything right. The people who do well are people who can look ahead and say, 'This is what we're going through now, it's happened in the past and I've gotten through it and I'll work through it this time, too." There are so many events that are going to impact you as a futures trader. I don't care who you are, you can never hope to always be on the right side of the market, but you can't let being wrong destroy your confidence. Keeping your balance goes back to putting in your time, doing your work, being a professional about it, and invariably, you'll get yourself turned around. I don't think from a war story standpoint you can gloat too much about your successes, and I don't think you can get too down on your defeats. You're going to have a heck of a lot of both of them. We've gone through a major drought in 1983, Chernobyl in 1986, another drought in 1988, a flood in 1993, and another drought somewhere in between there. Events like these are always going to be there. The thing that gives me hope, the thing that makes me feel confident about the future, is that as long as we have these kinds of vagaries in the market, these uncertain times, there's always going to be a need for the futures markets and there's always going to be an opportunity to make money. If everything were set, always the same, there would be no place for us in this industry. *We profit from the unexpected.* That's one of the reasons I look forward to each day when I get up to go to work. That sums me up.

Is there a way young people can tell if this business is really for them?

Well, like I just said about myself, you have to look forward to coming to work. You have to look forward to coming down here and seeing what opportunities are going to present themselves for that day. When you hate Fridays and look forward to Mondays, then I think you've really arrived. You don't get to where you feel that way, however, until you have some successes. If you're always getting cuffed about the ears, you aren't going to feel that way.

Is there anything you wish you would have been told when you started in this business more than twenty years ago?

If you're in your twenties, try to get clients who will still be with you when you're in your forties. Have that as your objective. That doesn't mean you don't want to solicit people who are older, but go into it with the idea that you'll still have these people fifteen, twenty years down the road. Give them the care and consideration that a goal of a long-term relationship would involve. If you approach it this way, it will be evident to them. As I said, if you approach them thinking you're going to make a quick turn commission on a trade or two, it's no good.

Can you think of any mistakes you've made in your career that maybe people reading this chapter can learn from and avoid?

Don't react to each day's information. Do your homework each day, each night and don't be too concerned with short-term swings.

Any final comments, Bucky?

Just a couple comments about working out. There are two reasons for working out. Actually three. One, I think it relieves stress and I think you have to have some stress relief other than alcohol. Two, when you get older, if you feel bad, you can't think as well. Three, and probably the most important, if you are consumed with the markets and that is what you're doing most of the time, if you have something you can do to get away from it, even for an hour or an hour and a half, it refreshes you to come back. Morning exercise can also give you a good frame of mind to come into the office and start to trade. If you roll out of bed, and get there and you're tired, it's no good. You get energy from physical activity.

Steve Solomon

Prudential Securities Incorporated
New York, New York

Steve, what's your background?

John, I was born in New York City, in the Bronx, in a middle-class neighborhood. I was an only child, played lots of sports growing up, and was pre-dental in college.

Where did you go to college?

I went to Farley Dickinson. After pre-dentistry, I planned to go on to Columbia Business School and study hospital administration. Instead, I was called into the army during the Vietnam war. After I got out of the service, I had to shelve my plans for graduate school because my father had just passed away. I had to earn money immediately, so I went to work for Xerox.

How did you get into the futures business, Steve?

It may sound strange, but this is really how it happened. One day, I saw Jack Dreyfus, one of Wall Street's giants, walking down the street, and I simply walked up to him and asked if he would please give me five minutes of his time for some advice.

I asked him, as head of the Dreyfus Fund, a leader in medical research, and as a visionary, what he would do if he were starting all over again. He said, "Wall Street's been very good to me; I'd do it all again, and I believe it would be a good place to build a career." I said, "Mr. Dreyfus, Wall Street's a big place. If someone had a few breaks and got lucky, what's a good area to get into that isn't too crowded?" He said, "Well, there's something called commodities which could have a great future. They have great potential for dynamic growth." When I asked him where I should start, he suggested, "Why don't you go over to Merrill Lynch?" I went over to Merrill and got in to see the office manager, John Conheeney, who went on to become Chairman of Merrill Lynch Futures. I told him how I introduced myself to Jack Dreyfus on the street and asked his advice. I think Conheeney admired my spirit, the way I approached Dreyfus, getting to him on my own. John agreed to give me a chance. He started me in their elite hedge unit, where I could learn from some of the best people they had in futures. There were six brokers, all of whom were major producers with major institutional clients—mainly hedgers rather than speculators. I spent five years there, observing and being taught by some of the smartest, most dedicated brokers in our business. What an education! What a foundation! After Merrill, I spent sixteen years with Hutton, until 1987 when I joined Prudential. I've been here ever since, working in several different areas such as: tax straddles, speculating, and hedging.

How did you build your business?

In the seventies, I decided to go after Japanese grain business. I put together a team of specialists: Carol Brookins, now President of World Perspectives; Ed Mader, the head of research, a grain specialist by background; Jim Harding on the floor of the Chicago Board of Trade; and an in-house meteorologist. I told prospects and clients, "For the price of the same commission dollar, you now can have a whole team working for you, instead of one broker sitting at a desk!"

Ours is a people business; people serving people. One of the many key people on our team here is Bruce Monaco, an extremely bright young man who joined me almost ten years ago. Bruce provides an intellectual dimension which "adds value" to the service we provide our clients.

So specialization and customer service was something you did early?

I tried to fill a void and create a niche for our team by providing outstanding, professional service.

Eventually, I got out of the grain part of our business because, after a period of inflation and runaway grain and sugar markets, I saw a change. It was pointed out to me by some clients who were seeing a move toward financial futures and currencies. Because of this, I quickly began shifting the direction of my business toward the financials, and got a foothold before other people did.

Steve, what about goals? Any comments to young brokers about setting goals?

Set goals that are attainable. Do not set goals that end up in disappointment. Don't overreach.

Do you have specific goals?

Yes, I have goals—attainable goals—not those that are way out of reach; otherwise, I would get frustrated or do the wrong thing along the way.

Steve, do you still prospect?

John, honestly speaking, I'm still very insecure. At the end of each year, I believe I can never have a year like the one before; therefore, I'm obsessed with prospecting after I'm sure the clients are well taken care of. Clients first, prospects second. Also, I only accept good clients. Even way back, pretty much, I only did business with good clients, and *whatever success I have, I owe to our clients. Our clients' success became our success.*

Instead of feeling intimidated, I have always gravitated toward people smarter than myself. I tell that to everybody. I would say that's the highlight, if you put one thing about me in your book. You should talk about the fact that I owe all my success to my clients. What I mean by that is, by having these brilliant customers, truthfully, as they got bigger and bigger, I was the lucky recipient of more and more good business. But after all that "getting," you have to give back something, too.

What does "giving back" mean?

It means a lot of different things. I like reciprocity, and it comes in many ways. It could come when someone who's been good to you for a long time is hurting and just lost a job at another firm. You make sure your friend doesn't flounder, you help where you can. Typically, I don't walk away from traders in a troubled trading climate when their basics are intact, such as strong ethics and good trading skills, qualities that are not easy to come by. It is important to stand by a trader who maintains these traits and survives until things become clearer. Life is give and take. It can't can't be a one-way street.

Also, you have to be there for young kids in the business. You have to be there for the charities. If people have put a lot of money in your pockets, you have to give some to the community. You have to be good to the people who are working for you. That's how I feel about give-backs. Some customers fall on hard times. When they call you, do you take their calls, or do you say, "I'm out to lunch," because they can't give you any business. You're supposed to be there for people because they were good to you through the years.

Steve, back to prospecting for a minute. What do you say to a prospect?

I'm a more negative sell than a positive sell to prospects.

I talk about risk control and money management before I talk about possible profits. I make someone aware of how we hopefully will deal with risk before we talk about reward. *Prospects should be made aware of all the negatives first.* If you meet prospects who really haven't had experience, even though they may be sincere and well-meaning, understand they haven't experienced some of the dilemmas that lie ahead and talk about them.

I think the third-party sale is the best sale, so hopefully someone will speak on my behalf before I ever speak to the prospect. Usually it's because they've known me for a while. It's like fixing someone up with a blind date: if you know both people, there is a good chance it might succeed, and if you know only one of the people, there is a good chance it might not. If you don't ask, you won't receive, so I often ask my biggest friends in the business, "By the way, do you know any great managers out there who may be about to leave their current situations to start their own firms?" I try to get in at an early stage with people who are special. Once they have all the money raised or once they put their whole group together, everyone comes knocking on their doors. It's important to be there at the beginning, to hold their hands and prove yourself to those people. Don't ever say you'll do things and then not do them. You must be there for them, constantly, with real help and in-depth service, not lip service. If you promise, you've got to perform.

Are you persistent?

I'm very persistent. I'm not a pain in the butt, but I am persistent. In other words, if someone says, "Steve, enough," then I back off. I'm not the type who will call someone five times a week. I don't mean persistent like that. I mean, if there's a good trader I'm selling, raising money for, I might talk about that trader for the next year on every trip to Europe. I'll go back, I'll talk again, I'll send a fax, I'll call, I'll send a chart, I'll go see those prospects again. I keep that trader's name in front of the people.

How about servicing an account? Any special work habits?

I've always overstaffed to make sure no one could ever say I was shorthanded because people were on vacation or out sick. *Clients don't want to hear the phone ring five times. Also, each customer wants something different.* No two customers are alike. What's important to one client is unimportant to the next. *You have to make all customers feel they're special because they are.* You have to gear your service to every person based on individual needs. You must do your best to hand-tailor your operation to the customers' needs. If you can't do it, if you can't supply customers with what they are hoping for, what they need, what they want, then you're better off passing on the business instead of taking on business you can't handle properly.

Also, we must be as professional as possible in every area we can control. For example, consistently accurate paperwork is crucial. Clients have more than enough to deal with in the markets without having to be subjected to the infuriating aggravation of bad paperwork. Bad paperwork drains mental, physical, and emotional energy, and there is simply no room for it, no excuse for it, in our business!

We try hard and our clients know we care. Also, there's a *quid pro quo*; the customer has to feel there's a fair balance. If you're deriving substantial income from a customer and you give skimpy service in return, it can't work.

What do you do to stay knowledgeable?

Truthfully, most of what I know about the world and the business really comes from our clients. *Our clients are the most knowledgeable investors and traders in the world, so by osmosis, I learn something.*

Bob Slotnick (Steve's associate, whom Steve had invited to sit in during the interview): May I comment on one thing? Earlier, you asked about work habits. Steve's work habits usually start with getting up early and having breakfast with a client. . . .

Do you have breakfast with clients often?

Probably four mornings a week.

Bob: And he ends his day at ten o'clock at night when he finishes having dinner with yet another client. He tells clients, if he hasn't gotten to them during the day, to call him at home between ten-thirty and midnight. He's usually on the phone until twelve-thirty.

Steve: That's true. Not to mention in my car. My car phone bills are over two thousand dollars a month.

Steve, if you had two or three pieces of advice to give to a futures broker, what would they be?

Try to specialize. Today's environment is not like it was ten years ago. What worked in the past won't necessarily work now or tomorrow.

Most importantly, be honest. Above all, never feel pressured into misrepresenting or misstating, even to yourself, much less to your customer. To be honest, I guess we've done between twenty and thirty million dollars in commissions year after year. That's a lot. That has happened by having good, solid customers. Right now, the money management component of Wall Street has just gone through a very rough year. These are tough times, and when times get tough in any cycle of life, you must continue to do all the right things so you're still around for the good times. You have to be known as a stayer, as a survivor. It's important to withstand the test of time. By being a survivor, by lasting, you automatically get to know more people, have more experiences, and then, if you've done your job well and consistently over the years, things start to fall into place.

When you're starting out a new company, a new career, it's normal not to know exactly which path to take. What seems so confusing today becomes obvious five years from now. John Conheeney told me when I first started out: "Steve, it's going to take you at least five years to avoid the temptations, the pitfalls, the corner cutting, all the things that could befall a young person in this business. If you can survive at least five years and keep your nose clean, you have a chance to really do well in this business, but most brokers won't survive even those five years." Then, the other thing is also to recognize your own abilities and lack of abilities. If you can't do really well, maybe you're better off doing something else. You know whether you're doing well. When you're a broker, a money manager, the bottom line is very clear. You know whether you did a great job, a good job, a mediocre job, or a poor job. Poor and mediocre are unacceptable.

Steve, anything else, any final comments you'd like to add?

I like this business. I love it. I love what I do. I wouldn't know what else to do if I had a chance to do anything I wanted. To me, this business was made for me because I love people, so I spend my time with people. To me this is fun. To some other people, it's a long battle. I don't look at it as a battle, but I'm also not saying I go home happy every single night, either. But most days I do.

Steve, as I look around your office, it's nice, but not opulent. You're not a material guy?

I don't want to go that far and misrepresent. I do drive a Bentley.

You've earned it. You've come a long way . . . by the way, do you ever go back to the old neighborhood?

Not in my Bentley, I'll tell you. Gotta run. Thanks.

Stuart A. Vosk

PaineWebber Incoporated
Farmington Hills, Michigan

Stu, please tell us about Stu.

I grew up in Michigan. Studied accounting in school. Worked for a CPA firm, wrote software for tax packages. Wanted to get out from behind the desk. Tried sales, liked it. Sold mutual funds, insurance, then futures. Been selling futures for about twenty-three years now.

I mentioned that I wanted to get out from behind a desk. I firmly believe that's what any futures broker or equities broker needs to do, especially to build his business. He needs to go see people. I think face-to-face selling in the insurance business was probably the greatest sales training anybody could ever get.

What did you learn from that sales training?

I learned to listen, and how to identify clients' needs. *Everybody's needs are different.* Write those four words on a piece of paper. Tape it where you see it every day. Every broker has in mind what he wants to tell prospects, and usually, it's the same thing for every prospect. That's wrong. You must tailor your sales efforts to fit each prospect's needs, and as I said before, everybody's needs are different.

Any advice about listening? When we survey people who have been prospected by futures brokers, most of them complain the broker does not listen.

Well, I have a problem in that I do cut people off sometimes. I'll ask them the question, they'll start answering, and as they're answering, I feel like I know what they're going to say and I start talking again helping them with their answers, which is absolutely wrong. You shouldn't do that. The best way to listen is to ask a question. Get the answer, ask more questions. Just keep asking questions until you know the prospect. This way you can decide if he would make a good client.

Really? What do you find out?

The prospect didn't have as much money as he said he did, or he didn't have the risk-tolerance for futures. Perhaps he would have been a problem, blaming losses on someone other than himself, taking no responsibility for his actions.

How can you tell from the first, second, or third meeting that somebody's not going to take responsibility for their actions or doesn't have the stomach for risk?

You probably can't until he actually starts trading. Sometimes you can—it's blatant. The prospect will say, "Oh, gees, *how* much? I can lose *five thousand dollars?*" Then you know you don't want him as a futures client. Sometimes the prospect will say, "Twenty grand, no problem." Still, you have to wait until he starts trading to find out what he's really like, which is why whenever I trade a new client—I don't care how much money he has—I always start him very small. I take his temperature in the futures market to see if he can handle it, winning or losing. If he can't, I close the account.

And you have closed accounts?

I've said "no" to many people over the years. You say no because they don't have the risk-tolerance or the emotional stability or the money. They're going to disrupt my business too much. A speculative futures trade is a business transaction: it either works or it doesn't work. If it doesn't work, then try another one.

Where do you get your leads?

I have always looked for businessmen. Entrepreneurs. I'm not as interested in an executive who works at some giant company or in doctors or lawyers. I want people who own their own businesses. They make business decisions every day. Every day is a risk for them. They have the tolerance, probably the money, and they're great clients.

Where do you find them?

Business directories.

Stu, what do you try to accomplish with the first phone call?

I want to see if the person is receptive to futures trading, and receptive to me. You need to try to establish income, liquid net worth, risk-tolerance, age maybe, education, sophistication, if the person can make his own decisions.

How did you build your book?

I worked seven days a week, probably fourteen hours a day when I started in the business.

Talk about getting started.

I got a list of people who had responded to ads. I was hungry, I came into the office every day and worked from seven in the morning to after nine at night and then went home and did some paper work. I did it for several months. I must have had sixty clients, but they were all small clients.

Stu, in addition to business directories, did you use any other lists?

Yes, there are list brokers all over who sell them; you can buy a list of people who subscribe to chart services, who have bought investment software, books about futures, and so on. A lot of commodity brokers like lists of gamblers who take junkets. I don't. I want businessmen. I want small businessmen. I want a person who knows how to make business decisions, is capable, likes to take risks to make money, takes responsibility for his actions, and can make a quick decision. Somebody who's not going to make me call back twelve times before he says "no." I'd just as soon have a "no" on the first call. In fact, I'd rather have a "no," than a "maybe."

When you worked all those hours, what were you doing on Saturdays and Sundays?

I was still on the phone. The funny thing is, the earlier I called people, the more impressed the people were. Most brokers don't want to call early in the morning because they're afraid the person is going to get upset. I found that the people I talked to, they'd say, "Boy, you're up awful early," and I'd say, "Hey, that's our business. The commodity business is worldwide, and it never sleeps."

How do you get new business today?

I ask for referrals. And I prospect some of my old clients.

Talk about going back to your old clients.

If I was lucky enough to have the right kind of client in the first place, I had someone who realized that if he lost money, it wasn't necessarily my fault. Brokers do the best they can. Brokers want their clients to make money because if the client makes money, the broker makes money. But you lost, okay. So you keep in touch with these people, you know what they're interested in, you just call them back. I have people who haven't traded for maybe two or three years, and I'll call them and often get them right back. *It's much easier to deal with someone you've dealt with before than to find somebody new.*

Can you tell me a little about the nature of your business?

All spec. Almost always has been. I've probably had three or four hedge clients in my entire life.

Is your business mostly in the Detroit area, or all over the country?

I think I'm pretty localized now. It used to be all over the country.

Do you have a minimum account size?

I try for fifty thousand dollars, I may open an account for less, it depends.

Any advice to new brokers about minimums?

Well, at first, they are probably going to have to accept smaller accounts. A fifty thousand dollar account is a nice account, but in the beginning they will gladly accept ten thousand dollar accounts. They have to start somewhere. What I say to people who don't open with as much as I want is, "Well, John, just make me this promise. If we do this and this works out well for you, I'm going to ask you for two things. I'm going to ask you for some of your friends' names, and I'm going to ask you for some more money." If he's never traded, I'm going to start him out small anyway, so I don't need a lot of money. Then if we start making money, I'll ask him for more, reminding him it has to be risk capital.

Stu, anything else about prospecting?

Never ever stop prospecting. I have over the years, and had some pretty bad years because of it. You know, you take a bad hit in the market, you lose some clients, you don't have anybody in the pipe line, and your production goes down. In addition to prospecting, I keep working trying to be the best broker I can.

How do you improve your skills?

Like any other broker would do, I guess: education, reading, studying, software, computers, looking at different systems, money management. I think education is probably the most important thing. Many people can sell. Not many people can handle the futures market. It's a tough market. Emotionally tough, physically tough, and mentally tough. Tough market.

In the educational process of learning how to trade, what are some examples of your resources?

Read all the books that are out there. The first one that I read was all about charting, written for stocks. I read almost everything else I could get my hands on since then about futures markets. Got into computers. I was using CompuTrac maybe ten or twelve years ago. I'm sure I wasn't one of the first users of CompuTrac, but I had my old Apple 2e out there, cranking out the numbers a long, long time ago. This has just come to me the last few years: the broker has to be comfortable with some kind of a system. It can be a fundamental system, it can be a technical system, or a combination—doesn't make any difference—but you've got to be comfortable with something that you think will do your client some good. Otherwise, the client is going to hear the insecurity in your voice when you're talking to him over the phone. He's going to know you don't know what you're talking about. Another thing, I'll have clients call me up who say, "I think soybeans are going up." I say, "I think they're going down." I give him my reasons, he gives me his reasons, and we'll say, "Let's forget the trade." We do a lot of that, talking each other out of trades.

What about money management? Could you talk about that a little?

Money management is very easy to talk about, but very hard to do. Some of the rules are "Don't lose more than five percent on any one trade," five percent of what's in your account. It's very, very hard because if the client or the broker isn't disciplined and didn't put in the stop when the trade was put on, as you see the loss growing, you're less inclined to get out or put in a stop after the trade is on. First of all, the broker doesn't want to say to the client, "I thought this thing was going to lose a thousand bucks—we're out five grand." The client, once he's lost five thousand doesn't want to say, "Gee, let's take the loss." They're both going to sit on it and wait to get it back, and of course, they never do. *So money management is the key to survival in this business, but it's tough. You've got to have some kind of a system of money management and stick to it.*

Let's go back to prospecting. If you were teaching a class of young brokers and the topic was prospecting, what would you say to them?

Be qualified to speak of what you speak. Know your product. Many brokers I've observed start selling a product, without really knowing what the product is. They haven't done the research, they're relying on somebody else to do it. The broker's got to do a little bit of research. He's got to know what he's talking about, really know it. It hurts all of us if there are a lot of brokers running around not knowing what they're talking about.

What other advice do you have for young brokers?

Know your prospect. You do that by asking questions. One of the things I do is push losses all the time when I'm prospecting. What I say is, "Of the people who trade futures, eighty-five percent or so lose." The prospect will say, "Then why do you want me to trade?" I say, "Well, maybe we can be part of the small group that makes money from the big group that does lose." Be honest, emphasize losses, margin calls, limit moves against, all the bad things that can happen, and if he's still interested, then you've got yourself a great prospect.

When you tell him all the negatives, aren't you afraid you're going to turn him off to the point where you'll lose him as a prospect?

No, if I lose him, I lose him. I would've lost him as a client after the first trade. Or the second trade. Whenever he took a loss, I would've lost him anyway.

You mentioned honesty earlier. What would you say about how it applies to the business of being a futures broker?

It's of the utmost importance. Besides, the client will see through any dishonesty. *I've said "no" to more trades than I've said "yes" to.* A lot of times, clients will call up and say, "I just heard on the news that such and such is happening. Why don't we buy some gold?" There is a sure commission for me. I don't have to do a thing. I didn't even have to solicit the order, but if I don't like the trade, I'll say no. I'll say, "First of all, if you heard it on TV, it's probably too late. Who'd you hear it from, the nightly news? How much do they have in the gold market?" That way, when I have what I feel is a good trade and call them up, they'll be more likely to do it, because I'm not a guy who just peddles trades.

How do you service an account?

I just talk to them all the time. Even if I don't have a trade idea for them, I call them up just to see how they're doing. I really care for my accounts, and I know they care for me. Maybe they do business with me six months out of the year and six months they don't because they're busy doing something else. Maybe they farm. I talk to them at least every month, just to chat.

Anything else about servicing an account?

Educate them. I like to educate my clients. Whatever system or technique I'm following, I educate my clients so they know what I'm doing. I recommend books to them, sometimes I buy them a book and send it to them. We discuss different systems. A lot of them are into computers. Most of my clients are familiar with computer software, so we can look at charts together.

Can you think of any books you've liked and can recommend to the readers of this book?

Yes, one of John Murphy's books, *Analysis of the Futures Market*. It's a technical book, and it talks about most of the systems that are out there. Explains them very nicely, what they are, why they may or may not work. I liked that book more than any commodity book I've ever read, and I bet I've read a hundred. I've got a pretty good collection.

Any books or tapes on selling you'd recommend?

There was a book I read when I first started selling called *The Five Great Rules of Selling*. That was a pretty decent book. I got into *The Power of Positive Thinking* and Napoleon Hill.

Stu, what about getting known in your marketing area?

I taught some night classes for a while. That was pretty good, I would recommend that to brokers. *I'd teach a night school class, have twenty students. Of those students I'd get ten clients.*

What was the topic of the class?

How to trade futures. The problem was that most of those clients were not really the kind of clients you're aiming for. They were the people who could only afford to risk five or ten thousand dollars. I also received some very good referrals from those smaller clients, and some of those smaller clients became bigger clients.

Work habits. What should they be for new brokers to be successful?

As a rookie, you've got to work all the time. Morning 'til night, day in and day out. Like a doctor, you've got to be on call whenever, because you are handling people's money. If somebody calls at two-thirty in the morning because they're worried about a trade, you had better be nice to the guy at two-thirty in the morning. As you get older and more sophisticated clients, it won't be as tough. You can take a little bit more time off, but not in the beginning. *It's the easiest way to make a good living as long as you are willing to work hard, very hard.*

This business has ups and downs. How do you get back in step if you're down?

You just do it. You pick up the telephone, you call people. You know, that's a great time to call some of your old people. Even if they don't trade, it gets you back into the swing of things, it gets you used to talking to people again. You remember some of the fire you used to have. It can be like that again. Old customers are easier to call than cold calls. Just say, "Gee, your kids are in college now. Last time we talked they were in high school" or whatever. *But if you're down, you can't talk to prospects. You've got nothing to say to them, and it's going to come through in your voice.* Read something like Napoleon Hill again, if you're not too old or too burnt out to take it to heart. I read a book not long ago by Deepak Chopra. Fabulous book, as far as I'm concerned it's a life-changing book: *Ageless Body, Timeless Mind.* Chopra believes your mind can cure many more things than medicine can.

Any pitfalls younger brokers should beware of?

Yes, yes, yes. The biggest pitfall: letting accounts get into trouble. Stop them before they get into trouble. That's the bane of the industry. You can't have debits, you must meet margin calls. You must use stops. You know, the whole money management thing. Before I put on a trade for the client, I'll tell them, "This looks like a pretty good trade to me. I think the chances of winning might be fifty-fifty. If we're right, I think we'll make three thousand. If we're wrong, I think we'll lose one thousand. Do you like that trade?" "Yes, I do." "Okay, we'll buy it here, here is our stop, we don't move this stop." "Okay, buy." The trade either works or it doesn't. End of story.

Stu, any final thoughts?

If you look at life, it isn't the goal that's important, it's the journey. When you reach the goal, you've got nothing else, it's over. So the important thing to me is to be always on that journey, never to reach the end. My journey is the intellectual pursuit of these markets. That's the important thing. The journey for me is fun.

You'd better love the business because it's much too hard a business to be in if you don't. John, as you can tell, I love this business. I really do.

This stuff is in your blood, Stu.

If they cut me open, they'll find soybeans.

800-832-6065